Masterpieces of Modern
Architecture

M. AGNOLETTO ▫ F. BOCCIA ▫ S. CASSARÀ ▫ A. DI MARCO ▫
G. ROSSO ▫ M. TAGLIATORI

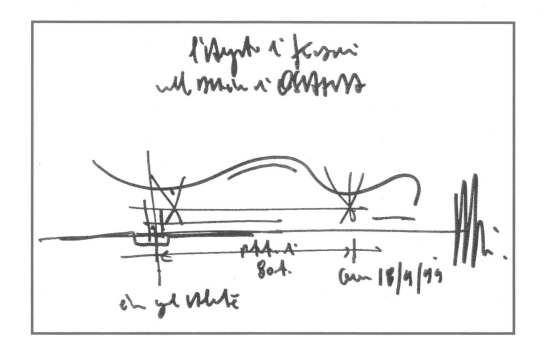

METRO BOOKS
NEW YORK

CONTENTS

TEXTS
Matteo Agnoletto
Francesco Boccia
Silvio Cassarà
Alessandra Di Marco
Guya Elisabetta Rosso
Marco Tagliatori

EDITORIAL PROJECT
Valeria Manferto De Fabianis

EDITORIAL COORDINATION
Novella Monti

GRAPHIC DESIGN
Paola Piacco

TRANSLATION
Catherine Bolton

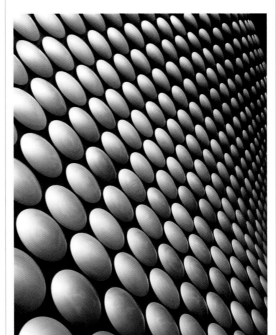

1 One of Piano's sketches depicts the typical cross section of the Kansai Airport Terminal.

2-3 The Nardini spheres or bubbles, designed by Fuksas, have a dazzling futuristic appearance.

© 2006 White Star S.p.A.

This 2006 edition published by Metro Books,
by arrangement with White Star S.p.A.

Metro Books
122 Fifth Avenue
New York, NY 10011

ISBN-13: 978-0-7607-8239-2
ISBN-10: 0-7607-8239-3

Library of Congress
Cataloging-in-Publication
Data available

Printed and bound in China
3 5 7 9 10 8 6 4

Color separation by CTM, Turin

PREFACE

In its own way, this book represents an era and probably – in a strictly chronological sense – a century. I say "in its own way" because other buildings could unquestionably be included in this series. Just as unquestionably, however, they would not alter it. Including other works would merely add buildings and images to a list that, like anything else, is perfectible, but whose sequence allows readers to follow an architectural path that is extraordinarily rich and varied, despite the recurrent presence of several materials that bear witness to an era. Equally, it allows readers to take an in-depth look at the difficult topic of architectural design in our day and age. This book examines 44 works that been divided by continent, but they reflect a world united by design that is less and less "territorial" and increasingly comprehensive. These projects straddle the end of the 20th century and the beginning of a new century that, with the exception of very few structures, is still too young to be characterized. What links them is the fact that they are "architectures" and represent a universal condition – that of manmade structures – regardless of their geographical location. As a result, they represent both the absolute and the relative, the mark of existence bearing witness to a reality that strives to achieve an "eternal present" (borrowing from Giedion) and challenges the fourth dimension – time – regardless of where the structure is built: in Europe, Africa, China, Australia, the United States, and South America. In other words, right around the world.

The globe is crisscrossed by these images and is often characterized by the works of the same architects in far-flung geographical areas. Though this kind of situation has existed since ancient times, today it is extremely facilitated and widespread. Its common thread involves simplifying the set of complexities that each project entails and attempting to resolve seemingly different themes that have become universalized in climates and terrains that are dramatically different yet somehow extraordinarily similar. The metropolitan environment is one example. Here, several buildings ostensibly strive to salvage the limitless mushrooming of constructions that are faceless and out of scale but that, at the same time, are also symbolic and epochal

representations: they are timeless witnesses. They also explore a formal world that the technological sophistication of familiar materials, like glass or metal, or new products (which are limited) can permit in a system (like the virtual one proposed by the media) that is marked by the hyperactive and global dissemination of images. These structures outdo themselves daily.

One of the greatest dangers for contemporary architecture lies in its confrontation with the media. At the same time, however, it also runs the risk of failing to carry out its function – regardless of whether it is residential or public – and of giving significant forms to spaces whose symbolic value often refers to societies that, though essentially homogeneous, are difficult to capture in forms that are significant or that will be meaningful over the long term, given the continuous changes they constantly face. By the same token, they are just as difficult to capture in forms that are alien to powerfully distinguished and unbending design philosophies.

It is intriguing to note the varied approaches that architects themselves take in defining design problems in different situations. For example, we can look at some of the works of Renzo Piano. Though his philosophy is generally quite technological, he has had to address highly differentiated settings that range from New York and London to New Caledonia, and that face completely diverse relational problems. We must also add that most of the works built today must deal with metropolitan settings with very similar problems in terms of identity and relations. These works do not limit themselves to serving as objects per se, with powerful individual, visual or monumental connotations, but spark reflection on their overall condition the moment they become "architecture." After all, architecture is the natural outcome – unconscious yet also cognizant – of the various disciplines and situations that converge in it, which are currently far more fragmented and changeable than in the past. This fragmentation often becomes tangible, as in the breakdown of form that is evident in the works of the Coop Himmelb(l)au group and emerges in the rapport and contrast with what already exists. Extant structures are incorporated or manipulated, emphasizing the

---

4-5 Foster's Hong Kong and Shanghai Bank stands out in the city's financial and architectural center.

6-7 Foster's dome over the Reichstag in Berlin reflects a formally cogent and spatially dynamic design.

8 The spherical form of the Shanghai International Convention SIC rises in the shade of the TV tower, facing the old Bund district on the opposite bank of the river.

9 The cladding of Selfridges Department Store in Birmingham is composed of over 15,000 disks that form an indeterminate mass.

11 The framework of the roofing of the TGV Station in Lyon, designed by Calatrava, reflects the finest Catalan tradition by incorporating astonishing spatiality.

dissimilarities and contradictions that constitute urban systems like those of Vienna and, more generally, of Europe. Here, the concept of architecture is recovered in disarticulation transformed into structure, and in the increasingly difficult notion of architecture as synthesis or as part of a set of relations that also encompasses the expressive mode tied to artistic experimentation and sculpture.

The problem involves redefining architectural expressiveness in a world in which standardization requires systems and potential interventions capable of reintegrating it in a circuit that has moved well beyond the formulations of the Modern Movement. In modernism, the relationships between art, technology and the built environment were perfectly identifiable, and visual roots determined the inherently valid and historically ascertained formulation of architecture. The sweeping modification – and even elimination – of artistic systems within the visual ones of information technology, coupled with the technical changes that have arisen, has effectively altered the set of certainties so arduously perfected by the programs of modernism. This has created sundry outlets for the creative subsystems that absorbed the problem of the aesthetics of design (in which aesthetics must be understood as the sum of the elements cited here).

Le Corbusier's *machine à habiter* – the industrially produced dwelling machine – was the culmination of the goal and the erudite potentiality of architecture, which remained only partially expressed and was suffocated by production that standardized function, neglecting its purposes in crumbling or vastly disintegrated urban systems. Postindustrial architecture has had countless benchmarks (yet also none at all), with fleeting and often anachronistic cultural underpinnings This has spawned enormous interest in the neutrality of machine-generated architecture, the kind founded on technology, and distinguished by mechanistic details and undifferentiated spaces. But it has also inspired examination of its own legacy. This legacy now pertains to the last century, but it must still be developed or at least enriched by the unexpressed potential that has never fully been accomplished. It is the legacy of the white prototypes – indeterminate from a design standpoint and marked by inexhaustible placeless potential – of Le Corbusier's houses, where everything seemed to reflect cogency, even when

incoherent. It involves materials, forms, strategies and the recovery of the ideal points of reference to which every historical period must defer. Richard Meier's church in Rome, illustrated here, is a perfect demonstration. In part, contemporaneity lives in the shadow of the same model. It too needs to be iconoclastic to be credible and deem itself as such. It is not the end of ratiocination that controls metaphor through geometry, but rather the extreme expansion of reason: like the windows of the Jewish Museum in Berlin or the abhorrence of vertical walls, transformed into alternative structural concessions. This architecture is no longer purely utopian like that of the Modern Movement. It is instead the partial realization of an idea that viewed the future as motion and transparency, speed and displacement. And contemporary architecture has all these features. It also has a totally different sense of limitation and scale that, alongside computers, has led to the adoption of design forms that shun typological continuity. Contemporary architecture represents the "here and now" in an astonishing way, and an overview of our continents confirms this, starting with Europe: Great Britain, France, Germany, Italy, Austria, Portugal, Spain and the Czech Republic. It is important to note that in more than twenty projects illustrated here – with the exception of the Berlin Philharmonie, which merits special attention not only because of its construction date (1963) but also the overall exceptionality of this work, and the Jubilee Church in Rome – masonry per se has dissolved to give way to more technological orientations.

The Lloyd's Building in London is somehow linked with the Pompidou Center in Paris and the dome of the Reichstag in Berlin, but also with Calatrava's Oriente Station and the roofing over the backbone of the routes at the Milan trade fair complex. They are the best solution to that type of problem, and as such they are perfect in their use of materials, but particularly the aspect that architecture has always yearned to achieve: transparency. Engineered architecture has proven to be the winning solution in the situations in which it is adopted. It makes specific choices vis-à-vis the urban layout and is set in the "neutrality" of a machine that has become an engine. Indeed, it moves beyond this neutrality through its inherent characteristics and its formal choices – grand but not complex – to follow in the footsteps of Europe's

---

12 Taut structures stand out against Paris' impassive Grande Arche, designed by Von Spreckelsen.

great urban infrastructures. In doing so, it has proven to be surprising ductile, not only in Calatrava's pseudo-Gothic revival but also in the presence/non-presence of the Berlin dome, reflecting ingenious insight and the solution to a problem that would otherwise have been insurmountable for a building that is so powerfully distinctive from a stylistic and historical standpoint. This architecture adopts a path that entails mechanical control over details, above and beyond the lack of spatial differentiation.

Space is how one encloses it, but it is also the display of a historicist and narcissistic mechanism that is its very soul, just as the soul of this architect steeped in engineering – like the great architects of the past – is quintessentially Catalan. And as we can glean from the Lisbon station, the secular cathedral of modern times and a paean to the monumentality of great structures. Libeskind and Gehry take a completely different stance. Their buildings – for example, the Jewish Museum in Berlin and "Fred and Ginger" in Prague – embrace the challenge of conceptual and real "distortion" of the history of architecture, a field they openly strive to negate – at least in terms of historical continuity and conceptual references.

Theirs is an architecture marked by a different kind of complexity. It is not mollified by the astounding impact of the structures, which it uses as a passe-partout for unpredictable spatial relations. Thus, the buildings themselves can no longer be interpreted through the simple standards of façade and roof, but in the totality of their self-construction – or its opposite. Consequently, their architecture anticipates innovative relationships with a system of forms that goes back to the sculptural "indefinite" yet also relies on information technology.

The quest for the poetics of space is left to the patient research of Richard Meier: to his relationship with cubist and constructivist collages, the sculptural purism of Frank Stella's works, and the oases of reason that strive not only to reflect but also to tame the surrounding dramatic urban and social complexity – simply because this is still possible. However, this architecture is also beguiling because it speaks to us of memory and of perfect relationships. Consequently, his use of white can also acquire polemical and innovative bents, without the stratagems of falling walls and lexical contortions that are so fashionable yet so short-

lived. These stratagems are also absent from the all-stone edifice of the Bibliotheca Alexandrina, designed by Christoph Kapeller of the Snøhetta firm. This measured work reconciles function, memory and cultural complexities, while also acknowledging "local" forms: the very forms that the hotel tower of Burj Al-Arab effaces in favor of self-promoting symbolism. In effect, this building could be located on any coast.

Nevertheless, Asia in general presents extremely interesting situations. Built in 1986, the Hong Kong and Shanghai Bank by Norman Foster, who also designed the city's enormous airport, was a watershed in the interpretation of the skyscraper. With Foster, the skyscraper was no longer viewed as an indefinite solid enveloped in continuous cladding, but as an organism displaying a structure and an articulation that accentuates a strange sort of horizontality, while also highlighting the vital system of motion, stairs and the sheer livability that pierces and crosses it. Foster's skyscraper is capable of creating a system of relations that this type of structure usually ignores and generalizes, altering the sense of place and its distinctive features. This is exactly what happens with other skyscrapers not far from here, which are simply intent on representing perfect execution without limitations as well as references that are not a typological iteration. To some extent, this can be seen in Cesar Pelli's Petronas Towers, whose record-breaking status – its height – is temporary but whose results are nevertheless unconvincing, despite recourse to a dual image.

The fact that technology is a tool that must be calibrated is also demonstrated in Asia by two of Renzo Piano's works, Kansai International Airport in Osaka and the Tjibaou Cultural Center.

The former is a masterpiece of the architecture of "non-places" – as airports have been defined – and the latter is a work that magnificently interprets the rapport between modernity and contextuality. The Tjibaou Cultural Center effectively questions the historical terms for evaluating works in pristine areas and it leads to the idea of reconsidering the possible use of materials and symbols, without indulging in concealment and camouflage. Moreover, it underscores the fact that materials do not determine the timelessness and modern qualities of a building: metal in the first case, wood in the second. Piano interpreted his commission

13 The curved white "sails" of Calatrava's Tenerife Opera House are powerful and aggressive in appearance.

based on construction possibilities, and in both cases the finished product enhanced the characteristics of existing structures.

This brings us to the New World, and our overview continues with a rather vague differentiation that is becoming obsolete. It involves the distinction between the philosophy of cement – essentially European and thus French – found in Canada and represented by Moshe Safdie's work, and the Angeleno approach of a Canadian constantly on the move: Frank O. Gehry. Safdie has long been committed to works with powerful urban significance, whereas the latter overturns the design language familiar to all of us. From residential structures to collective space, from the absolute destruction of traditional models to the experimental use of materials capable of responding to a formalism that broadens the old beam-and-pillar construction system, Gehry portrays a complex and emotional society for which nothing is certain any longer. This is what his architecture reflects and proposes, from Bilbao to Barcelona, Prague and Los Angeles: in its infinite expansion of horizontality, his work in Los Angeles is also the best place to grasp the interplay of architecture that captures the very soul of "de-urbanized" society. He does this by using supermarket materials, mesh and pre-cut wood, along with exorbitantly expensive titanium, the only material that can create the endless twisting of roofs and façades that has become his hallmark. Gehry shakes the roots of statics to the greatest physical limits, simulating structures frozen as they crumple and using the potential offered by computers to dissect a fluidity that would be impossible to govern otherwise. The panorama is extensive, of course, and there is much more to examine. We have the Guggenheim in New York, which joins Scharoun's building in Berlin and Niemeyer's works in Brasília to constitute the underpinnings of the history of the Modern Movement.

They enjoy a sort of geographical and territorial supranationality because they are inimitable and unique. Scharoun's concert hall was the first modern architecture to bring an individual slant to the standard rationalist approach towards designing a building as complex as the Philharmonie.

No more basic grids, rational structural matrices, right angles or flat roofs: Scharoun introduced "organized" structural disorder, pre-Gehryesque spatial complexity, undulating roofs and an extravaganza of dissonance and "harmonic" visual disharmony.

Even today, the auditorium is a masterpiece of the absolute appropriation of a space that, until then, had been congealed in the seating-orchestra-stage layout, according to a concept that, as Peter Eisenman affirms, seems to underscore that aesthetics cannot be the primary element of architecture but its consequence. This is not a building in the usual sense of the term, as noted by Bruno Zevi in his work on the spaces of modern architecture. But this statement can also apply to the Guggenheim Museum that Frank Lloyd Wright designed in New York, a building that is only a few years older than Scharoun's, as it was completed in 1959 after a laborious planning and construction phase spanning thirteen years. The Guggenheim is a benchmark in museum design, just as the Philharmonie is for concert halls. Anyone who examines the two cross sections immediately grasps the power of these groundbreaking architectures – the former expressionist, the latter organic – and all terms of reference fall sorely short in explaining them. The enormous internal spiral route – the kind generally used for parking garages but applied here to create an internal exhibition path (much to the dismay of the museum's curators) – creates a billowing, changeable space. The effect is one of esotericism that is enhanced by the dome. Though the dome is not the one Wright originally designed, it completely dissolves the appearance of the roofing, ensuring equally changeable interior lighting. The result is this "ineffable space" whose appeal goes beyond function and gives each visitor sensations and emotions comparable to those stirred by the great architectures of the past, from the Pantheon to Gothic cathedrals. The transparency of these structures can be found in the Metropolitan Cathedral in Brasília, designed by Oscar Niemeyer. In the surreal setting of the Brazilian capital, this architect successfully connects Western tradition with modern construction concepts in a deeply meaningful and enthralling natural setting.

Though the Square of the Three Powers leaves the eloquence of symbolism – or rather, of the manmade symbols of the Parliament complex – isolated on a platform adjoining the void facing the forest, the cathedral turns to Gothic memories and brings them into a structural concept that culminates with the enormous crown of this design: the interior. It lets the superiority of light inundate this space, allowing the interior to absorb brilliance or darkness or tropical storms: simply and extraordinarily, in a way that only architecture can express.

Silvio Cassarà

---

14 *Cavernous forms occupy the spaces of the atrium and the entrance to one of the rooms in the courtyard of Gehry's DG Bank in Berlin.*

16-17 *Gehry's Guggenheim Museum Bilbao explodes in an extraordinary array of forms.*

18-19 *The gallery of the Planetarium at Calatrava's City of Arts and Sciences in Valencia effectively splices two different buildings.*

Imperial War Museum North

MANCHESTER, UNITED KINGDOM

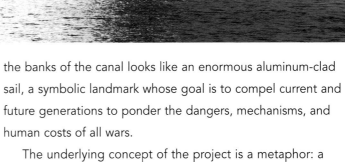

S lituated on the outskirts of Manchester, the Imperial War Museum North is England's first work by the American architect Daniel Libeskind. It rises along the Manchester Ship Canal at Salford Quays, an incoherent and fragmentary district made up of buildings that have gradually filled the voids left by the city's past as an industrial center.

Libeskind gained renown for introducing a critical and multidisciplinary language into architecture – his Jewish Museum in Berlin is emblematic – and in 1997 he won the design competition for the museum, which the city decided to build to commemorate Manchester's devastation during World War II. As is the case in Berlin, the outcome is a building whose symbolism is so powerful that it effectively disorients visitors the moment they enter. This impressive structure on

the banks of the canal looks like an enormous aluminum-clad sail, a symbolic landmark whose goal is to compel current and future generations to ponder the dangers, mechanisms, and human costs of all wars.

The underlying concept of the project is a metaphor: a world shattered by war and recomposed in a landscape of artificial ruins, and fragmentariness that also epitomizes the breakdown of the contemporary world. Global "deconstruction" is embodied by a building composed of three "shards" that, though simple in form, possess all the drama of the memories of those who have survived war. The three shards – Earth, Air, and Water – correspond to the spaces where the war was fought, and they interlock in dramatic tension that determines their specific functions. The feeling of disorientation that is evoked even from afar is

20 The deconstructed volumes of the Imperial War Museum overlook the Manchester Ship Canal, in a derelict area that was formed when the city's industrial sector declined.

20-21 The various parts of the museum are formed by the intersection of three large but fragmented structures that, according to Libeskind, stand for a world shattered by war. Earth, Air and Water Shards represent the spaces where the war was fought. The enormous museum completely dwarfs the surrounding buildings.

21 bottom The walkway of the Air Shard tower, which is 180 feet tall, offers a 360-degree view. The entire building is clad in aluminum.

DESIGN	CONSTRUCTION	DIMENSIONS	USE
D. Libeskind	1997-2002	Total area 96,875 square ft	History museum

Imperial War Museum North

magnified at the entrance to the museum, a winding concrete trench that perforates the largest section, a curved tower rising 180 feet over the entire complex.

After passing through an open-air foyer that inspires introspection, visitors enter the main pavilion, passing under a dramatic curved ceiling that follows the curvature of the Earth. This space evolves continuously and the layout is revealed through individual pieces that survived the irrational reality of which they were part. This is an order of irregular ideas of which space is the principal matrix, with bold sightlines and corners behind which symbolic objects like a Russian T-34 tank – still mud-splashed – seem to be waiting in ambush. Projectors have been set up to transform the space through 360-degree images, catapulting visitors into the very heart of combat.

To the left of the main entrance, an elevator rises diagonally inside the hollow sloped structure of the Air Shard to reach the observation platform, set at a height of 95 feet above the canal and affording a view of the skyline. The tower may be too unnerving for some, as the flooring is a metal grid that powerfully conveys the precariousness of the lives in the countryside below the bomber pilot. Calmness returns in the Water Shard, which extends along the canal, and houses the café, restaurant, bookshop and performance areas.

During construction of the Imperial War Museum North, major budget cuts reduced the original funding by about one-third. Nevertheless, Libeskind achieved an extraordinary level of quality in this work, which is destined to become a cultural dynamo for the entire region of Manchester. (Marco Tagliatori)

22 The museum, which cost 46 million euro (55 milllion dollars) to build, houses galleries devoted to British fighting tactics starting with World War I, and its goal is to encourage visitors to ponder the dangers, mechanisms, and human costs of war.

23 top A Harrier, the icon of modern technological warfare, juts out from the corner of one of the rooms.

23 center The exhibition layout is irregular, with objects set randomly in an attempt to represent what remains in the minds of those who have survived war.

23 bottom Enormous diagonal gashes – like wounds – form openings to let in natural light, taking up a concept that Libeskind also used at the Jewish Museum in Berlin.

24 top and bottom right Though the façades of this building are simple, its elevation demonstrates its full complexity, which stems mainly from the use of different heights. The central portion, made of glass, culminates in a clear barrel vault.

24 bottom left The new Lloyd's Building is set in a high-density and enormously complex urban fabric representing the remains of the ancient layout of the medieval city. This contrast is part of what makes this work so fascinating.

Lloyd's of London

LONDON, UNITED KINGDOM

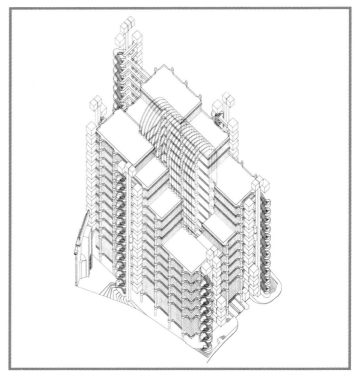

Designed for the world's most important insurance company, the Lloyd's headquarters is situated in one of the oldest districts in London, the heart of the city and the place where the Romans decided to establish their empire across the English Channel.

Because of its enormous growth, in just the past fifty years Lloyd's has had to renovate its headquarters three times, and this led to the need to design a new building that would respond to the company's requirements. The original building, dating back to 1928, was demolished to make room for the new structure. The Lloyd's Company, founded in the late 17th century as a coffeehouse where the members of different insurance organizations would meet to manage their business, is now one of the largest financial companies in the world.

In 1978 Richard Rogers won the commission to design the

building, following an initial selection of forty architectural firms, later narrowed down to six.

Rogers successfully incorporated the building within the historic fabric, creating maximum volume with respect to available area. At the same time, however, he did not alter the historic urban layout.

Steel and glass are the main materials used to build the new headquarters. However, unlike numerous 20th-century glass-and-steel towers whose main purpose is to dazzle the observer with gleaming windows and unusual forms, the building's essence is the outcome of function and the intensive use of technology.

In order to optimize function inside the building, the auxiliary systems were shifted towards the outside, permitting easy access and maintenance, and thus maintaining the space that would have been lost if they had been installed inside. The six service towers were set in the space left between the edges

DESIGN	CONSTRUCTION	DIMENSIONS	USE
R. ROGERS	1979-1986	TOTAL AREA 592,015 SQUARE FT	RESTAURANTS, CAFÉS, LIBRARY, SHOPS, LLOYD'S OFFICES

25 Richard Rogers' decision to install the ducts on the outside of the building – a concept he had already used for the Centre Pompidou, designed with Renzo Piano – gives the structure a distinctive appearance from all angles.

Lloyd's of London

26 Bringing the plant engineering structures to the outside exaggerates the building's high-tech aspect, creating a sense of astonishment and conveying the architect's brilliance. If we consider the fact that the building was completed in 1986, it is easy to imagine the uproar surrounding its inauguration.

27 top The Lloyd's Building was one of the first skyscrapers to invade the City, but other larger and more impressive buildings soon followed. Norman Foster's Swiss Re Tower stands out in the background. Though it is 18 years younger, its principles were inspired by Rogers' building.

27 bottom left In designing the Lloyd's Building, Rogers attempted to create a work that would exploit solar radiation for both lighting and heating purposes. This cross section, submitted for the competition, highlights the main features of the buildings.

27 bottom right The contrast between the Lloyd's Building and the surrounding urban fabric has a powerful impact due to the height difference, the use of materials alien to this setting, and the original and innovative forms that shape the exterior of the structure.

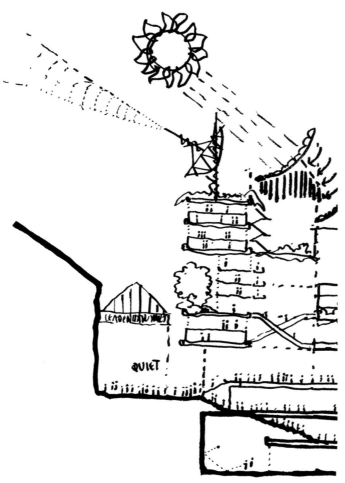

of the lot and the central part of the building. Three of them are designed chiefly as fire escapes, whereas elevators, heating and air-conditioning systems, and bathrooms are located in the other three. The building is accessed through the service towers; elevators and escalators are used for vertical movement. In case of emergency, the entire building – which can hold up to six thousand visitors – can be evacuated through the towers in just two-and-a-half minutes.

The towers rise to heights of six to twelve stories, according to the buildings around them: the tallest tower faces the taller adjacent buildings, whereas the shortest one is set alongside lower constructions.

By installing the service infrastructures on the outside, Rogers accentuated their role. For example, instead of

concealing the air-conditioning ducts within the building, he placed them on the façade, maximizing their size to make the function of the building itself evident.

This is one of London's first "intelligent buildings," so called because the interior incorporates technological elements that facilitate their management. Generally referred to as a building management system, this type of structure was based on the technologies available at the time it was built. As a result, it runs the risk of becoming obsolete within a short time due to fast-paced technological advances.

To avoid this problem, the architect chose to use modular auxiliary systems. This means that each one can be replaced or upgraded on site whenever the progress made in technology makes it possible or necessary.

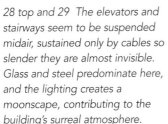
28 top and 29 The elevators and stairways seem to be suspended midair, sustained only by cables so slender they are almost invisible. Glass and steel predominate here, and the lighting creates a moonscape, contributing to the building's surreal atmosphere.

28-29 The massive presence of the structure inside the building is surprising, given the predominance of metal and glass on the outside. However, this "heaviness" is balanced by the bright airy atrium and the clear roof.

Lloyd's of London

In fact, the innovation of this building also lies in the fact that all the plants are easily accessible and the spaces devoted to them have been designed with an eye to the future, making it possible to replace all the technologies used with later ones.

From the moment Lloyd's drew up its list of objectives, it was clear that one of the main requirements was that the building would have to be operational for at least fifty years. As a result, its most important feature is adaptability. The basic structure was designed to last fifty years, whereas the air-conditioning system and communications network were designed for a shorter life.

Since the building opened in 1986, the layout of the floors and the systems engineering have changed several times to cater to the company's needs. Both the main body and the service towers are made of reinforced concrete. The main body was then enclosed in an independent curtain, composed of a technological wall that not only protects it from wind and rain, but also serves as an air conduit and insulation. The air space between the double-pane windows and the single-glazed cladding channels air from the roof to the ground. Moreover, because of its special composition the glass wall also filters light. The six towers are clad with stainless-steel fireproof sandwich panels, whereas glass structures were used for the elevators. The building is composed of a concentric gallery that rises 250 feet over a central atrium.

Instead of floors composed of anonymous hallways, closed doors, and blind, dark elevators, we find free floor plans, glass partitions that permit eye contact within the different offices and afford a sweeping view of the city, a set of open escalators

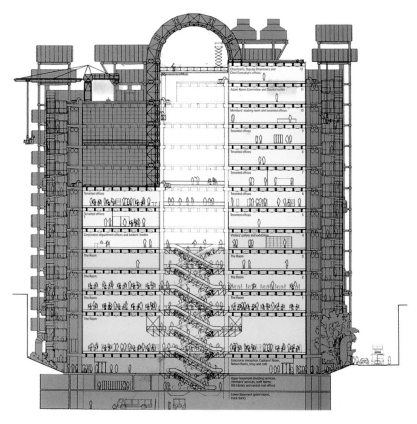

30 and 31 center The Underwriting Room is the heart of the building: this is where negotiations are held and deals are made. In the middle of this area, there are escalators that bring visitors up to the fourth floor and the Lutine Bell, which tolls good and bad news. The space in the Underwriting Room is partitioned to meet the needs of the brokers, who can rent a stall and furnish it as desired.

31 top The elevators in the service towers allow personnel to go to any floor, whereas the escalators go only as far as the offices on the fourth floor.

31 bottom The axonometric projection shows the placement of the service towers and the layout of the interior space allocated to the Underwriting Room.

Lloyd's of London

that cross the building, and glass elevators that whiz up and down the external towers, giving the building the appearance of something straight out of a sci-fi novel. The impression all this creates is one of a building seething with activity. Public venues such as the restaurant, café, shops and a library are on the ground floor. The "Lutine Bell" has been placed in the main atrium. The bell was from a cargo ship, insured by Lloyd's, which sank with its valuable cargo in 1799 and has become the symbol of the company. The bell, which was once used to signal bad news (one stroke) and good news (two strokes) about the company's activities, is now rung only for special commemorations. The enormous size of the atrium echoes the sound of the bell, which can be heard everywhere in the building. The heart of building is the Underwriting Room, located above the ground floor. This is where the various insurance brokers conduct negotiations. The brokers can rent one or more stalls and set them up freely based on their needs. The Underwriting Room has an open plan that is extremely flexible, and it can occupy an area of more than 204,000 square feet. It is set in the center of the building and its height crosses all the floors of the building. It affords a complete view of the entire building and, by the same token, virtually the entire building can observe what is happening in the Room. In designing the Room Rogers managed to recreate the same lively and productive atmosphere that was present in the 17th century at Edward Lloyd's coffeehouse. The innovative design of the Lloyd's Building in London has earned it numerous prizes, notably the one awarded by the Royal Institute of British Architects (RIBA) in 1988. (Alessandra Di Marco)

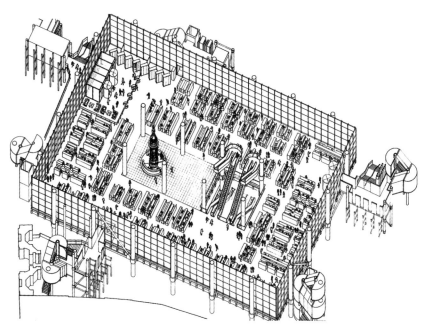

City Hall

LONDON, UNITED KINGDOM

32 top London City Hall is the headquarters of the Greater London Authority and of the offices of the Mayor of London. The amphitheater, an enormous outdoor space used for public events and concerts, is visible in the foreground.

32 bottom The terrace of London's Living Room faces the Tower Bridge.

33 A night view of the building reveals the interior, with the ramp connecting the different floors.

London City Hall is the headquarters of the Greater London Authority and home of the mayor, and was inaugurated on July 23, 2002 by Queen Elizabeth II and the Mayor of London, Ken Livingstone. The highly original design of the new building, which has been likened to the most diverse forms, is the work of Sir Norman Foster, of the Foster and Partners firm of architects.

The building is situated on the south bank of the Thames. The location was chosen from 55 possible alternatives in a contest to find the best site, considering the building's great evocative power within London's austere urban landscape, in direct contact with two of the cornerstones of the old city – the Tower of London and Tower Bridge.

However, the impact of such an important addition to the urban fabric reveals conscious determination and visionary genius in terms of design within an existing environment. The building has neither a front nor a back, but simply elusive views generated by the continuous rotation of the surface of a deformed sphere. It is not presented as a distinguishable geometric form, but draws its shape from the need to achieve certain environmental objectives, allowing considerable energy savings due its exposure to sunlight and the use of state-of-the-art engineering solutions. The glazed façades are not only related to the technological functionality of the design, but also symbolize the transparency of the democratic process and the accessibility of the city's administration to its citizens.

The profound innovation introduced by Foster lies in the sought-after and very conscious environmental sustainability of the design. Indeed, the British architect devised an integrated environmental control system in collaboration with the London-based design firm Arup Associates in order to optimize energy consumption, which allows City Hall to use only a quarter of the energy required by a normal air-conditioned building.

Computer simulation was used to model the behavior of the sunlight on the glazed surfaces, allowing optimum calibration of transparency and exposure. The southern side of the building features overhangs to shade it from direct sunlight, while the northern side is completely faced with transparent glass.

DESIGN	CONSTRUCTION	DIMENSIONS	USE
N. Foster	1998-2002	Total area 129,167 square ft	Headquarters of the Greater London Authority, Assembly Chamber, library, public offices

During the winter, heat is recovered from the outgoing air and recycled. In the summer, groundwater is pumped up from the water table to cool the air-conditioning circuits and is then channeled into the sanitation system, minimizing the building's water requirements. The building imparts the sensation of a light, open structure that is transformed throughout the day, passing from natural daylight, which is exploited on the inside, to artificial lighting that projects the image of its spaces towards the outside.

The most inspired interior feature is the 2400-foot spiral ramp that is open to the public and winds its way up to London's Living Room on the top floor, overlooking the Assembly Chamber and offering access to a panoramic terrace with splendid views of the skyline. City Hall's eleven stories cover an area of around 130,000 square feet and, in addition to the headquarters of the GLA, house public services, the mayor's offices and the Assembly Chamber, a public library, administrative offices and restaurants. Outside, a large amphitheater is used to host public events and concerts. This area can be reached from the basement level, which houses a restaurant and four meeting rooms and is accessible via another spiral ramp beneath the Assembly Chamber. (Marco Tagliatori)

34-35 Enormous glass walls – symbolizing the transparency of democracy – make the Assembly Chamber, on the ground floor, visible from the outside.
The walkway encircling this hall is usually open to the public.

35 top The ramp, which rises from the ground level to the upper floors of the building, resembles the one in the Reichstag in Berlin.

City Hall

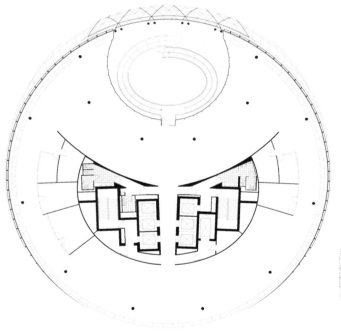

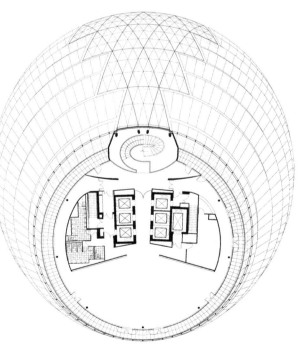

35 center The offices have been designed as flexible spaces that can be left open or divided into smaller areas using solid or clear partitions.

35 bottom left Plan view of the second level, with the Assembly Chamber, the spiral ramp, and the stairwells and elevators. The chamber, which can seat 250 people, can be arranged in various configurations to accommodate different kinds of

events. From the interior, there is a view of the Thames and the London skyline.

35 bottom right Plan view of the ninth level, with London's Living Room. This is one of the most popular party venues in London. From here, visitors can see the interior of the Assembly Chamber, whereas the terrace affords a stunning view of the city. The site for City Hall was chosen from 55 possible alternatives.

36-37 Located in the heart of the City, not far from the Lloyd's Building designed by Richard Rogers, the Swiss Re Tower has unquestionably become a landmark on London's skyline.

36 bottom The entrance to the tower is located in the square, where the first ring of the triangular mesh seems to bring the outdoors into the building.

37 top left The rapport between the tower and its urbanized setting is marked by divergence, as the tower differs enormously from its surroundings in terms of form, materials and height.

37 top right To design the shape of the building, Foster conducted studies on the turbulence skyscrapers generate in the space around them.

DESIGN	CONSTRUCTION	DIMENSIONS	USE
N. Foster	2001-2004	Total area 822,362 square ft	Shops, cafés, Swiss Re offices, office space leased to other companies, private restaurant

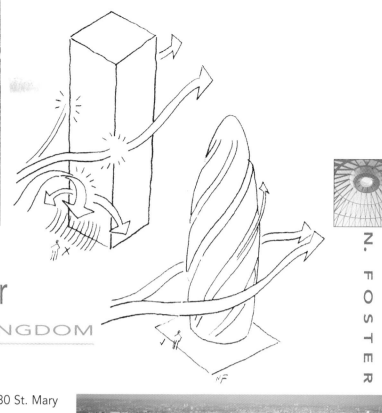

Swiss Re Tower

LONDON, UNITED KINGDOM

I ts official name is the same as its address, 30 St. Mary Axe, but it is widely known as the Swiss Re Tower, after the Swiss Reinsurance Company that commissioned it for its British headquarters. However, the moniker by which it has become famous is the "Gherkin," due to its evocative phallic architecture. It is one of the latest masterpieces by Sir Norman Foster, and in 2004 it won him the prestigious Stirling Prize, awarded by the Royal Institute of British Architects (RIBA) to the best new projects built in Great Britain or by British professionals in Europe. Foster's building was chosen over those of five other finalists.

The distinctive form of this skyscraper, set in the heart of the City, London's financial district, has consecrated it as a landmark. Indeed, its unique architecture makes it an immediately recognizable feature of the capital's skyline. However, the consensus is not unanimous, for some see the tower as an alien building out of context rather than a daring addition to the urban landscape. Nonetheless, the tower has already become an integral part of the city, despite the fact that its form has little in common with the surrounding buildings. The finished structure is the result of lengthy negotiations between the architect and the community, and the desire for change proved to be the dominant factor.

Despite its impressive size (590 feet high, with 40 stories covering a total area of 820,000 square feet), the Swiss Re Tower is considered London's first environmentally sustainable skyscraper.

Its aerodynamic shape minimizes wind loads on the building by encouraging air to flow around it, whereas its glazed skin allows the maximum use of natural light, aiding natural ventilation and reducing energy consumption by 50% compared to a traditionally built tower of the same size.

Furthermore, the offices offer unrivaled views over the city, as the exterior of the building is composed of 260,000 square feet of glass panels that satisfy the primary objective of creating a connection with nature, allowing its inhabitants to admire the surrounding urban landscape.

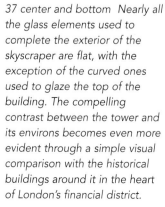

37 center and bottom Nearly all the glass elements used to complete the exterior of the skyscraper are flat, with the exception of the curved ones used to glaze the top of the building. The compelling contrast between the tower and its environs becomes even more evident through a simple visual comparison with the historical buildings around it in the heart of London's financial district.

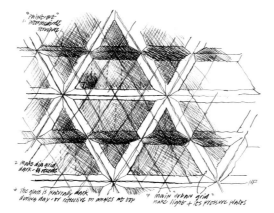

38 The shell is based on a structure that spirals upwards around the building. The use of glazing in different colors emphasizes this structural feature.

39 top and center The sketch and photograph clearly show the different lattices that compose the building.

39 bottom The sketch of the floor layouts demonstrates Foster's desire to create a structure in which the penetration of sunlight, and the circulation and exchange of natural air between the internal and external spaces play a fundamental role.

The 5500 triangular panels are arranged in a diamond pattern and their dimensions vary according to level. The panels are double on the exterior and single on the interior, creating a ventilated central cavity, where sophisticated devices control the amount of solar radiation, allowing a drastic reduction in the use of air conditioning. A diagonally braced steel exoskeleton was adopted in order to create column-free interior spaces.

The resulting office space occupies a net area of 450,039 square feet with a highly complex section, due to the fact that the various floors are subdivided into radial sectors that spiral towards the top of the building, thus creating a space with an extremely differentiated layout. Solids (offices, circulation shafts, etc.) are alternated with voids (hanging gardens, balconies, atria, etc.), aiding the natural ventilation of the building due to the pressure differentials created between the various floors. Every two or six floors, there are "sky gardens" created not only to oxygenate and purify the air, but also to act as a fire-barrier.

The typical office floor is divided into six rectangular blocks, in which triangular service areas are inserted. The spaces next to the skeleton, which lead to an atrium or a garden, are thus transformed into meeting and break areas. The offices of the Swiss Reinsurance Company currently occupy just a few floors in the building, whereas the others are available for rent only, and not for sale, in order to allow for future expansion of the company.

The functions housed within the building are not merely limited to the service sector. Indeed, the circular plan has been exploited to create a public space of approximately 21,500 square feet with shops, for the main purpose of integrating the new building with the surrounding area. The

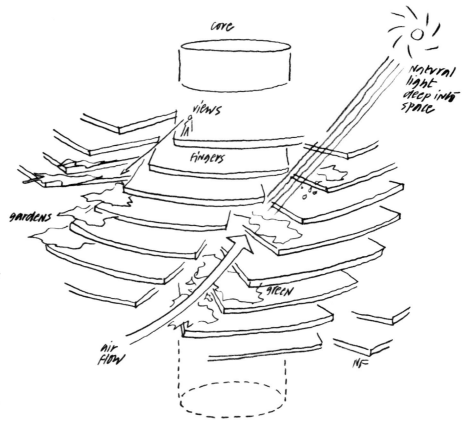

large glazed surface of the structure and its interior distribution features allow the plaza to make the most of solar radiation. In the attempt to make this covered space resemble a square, fully grown trees were planted in it and low stone walls were built to divide the area and to serve as benches. Beneath the glazed dome at the opposite end of the skyscraper, the 39th and 40th stories respectively house a restaurant and a bar, which boast a 360-degree panorama over the entire city. Conceptually the tower develops ideas

Swiss Re Tower

40 top The covered square is accessed through four revolving glass doors that control not only the people entering the building but also the elements.

40 bottom left A restaurant and lounge bar are located on the top floor of the building, under the glass eye. They are open only to those who work in the building and their guests.

40 bottom right Foster's theory on natural ventilation and lighting entailed extensive research into the shape of the glass panels, as well as their inclination, color, and opening mechanism.

41 At the balconies located near the shell, the boundary between ground and sky seems to vanish, and the juxtaposition of horizontal and vertical glazed surfaces forges a visual bond between the floors of the building and the exterior.

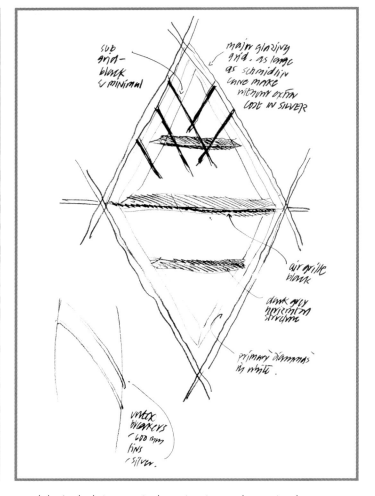

explored by Foster in the Commerzbank and, before that, in the Climatroffice project, designed with Buckminster Fuller, which suggested a new rapport between nature and the workplace.

In this case, the development of the diagonally braced structural envelope has allowed the creation of large, open spaces and a fully glazed façade, which opens up the building to light and the outside world. The atria and gardens on each floor visually link the inner space to form a series of informal break areas that spiral up to the top of the building. Despite its decidedly unusual appearance, the form and function of the structure generate an architectural organism that is well equipped to withstand the many kinds of static stress to which it could be subjected. The aerodynamic contour of the building is the result of a detailed study of progressive curves, analyzed and established using sophisticated parametric computer

models. Its bulging conical section instead permits the regulation of wind flows, thus reducing air pressure at the plaza level, while the spiral steel structure ensures greater energy efficiency and lighting intensity. The combination of the particular materials used, the futuristic shape and the qualities that make it an environmentally sustainable system have made the Swiss Re Tower one of London's landmarks. It is a clear example of the new conception of the skyscraper that has been establishing itself in recent years, where the building is no longer seen as a mere rectangular container that is divorced from its context and squanders resources. Foster himself maintains that only skyscrapers can solve the problem of urban development, without underrating their aesthetic role. Indeed, he claims that no other structure has a similar visual impact and the power to become the symbol, or icon, of a metropolis and its modernity, vitality and growth. (Alessandra Di Marco)

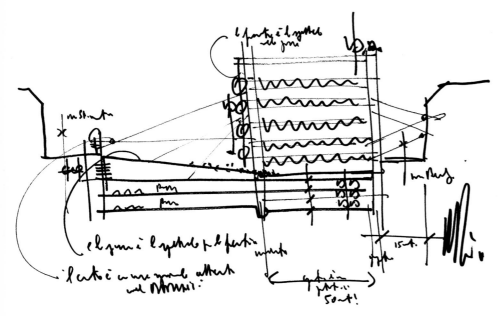

42 top The Centre Pompidou was designed as a machine of steel pipes dropped into the historic fabric of Paris. In Piano's sketch, the cross section demonstrates the building's relationship with the new urban plaza through a system of underground areas and floors above ground level that house the exhibition areas.

42-43 and 43 top In the final architectural solution, which altered the model that won the competition by adding the escalators in the middle of the façade, Piano and Rogers designed a single ramp that cuts diagonally across the front of the museum.

DESIGN	CONSTRUCTION	DIMENSIONS	USE
R. PIANO R. ROGERS	1971-1978 1996-2000	TOTAL AREA 1,076,391 SQUARE FT	MULTIPURPOSE CULTURAL CENTER AND MUSEUM

42 bottom The drawing shows the thirteen bays of the façade, punctuated by structural steel posts and the "crosses" of the tie rods, forming three orders that correspond to two floors.

43 bottom The plant engineering system of the Centre Pompidou literally clings to the back of the building.

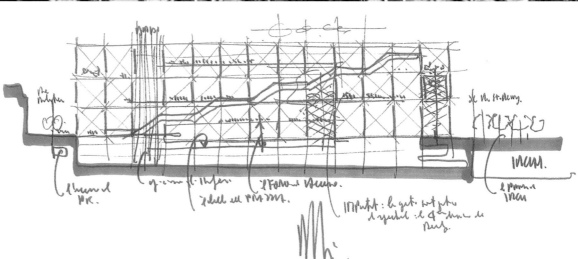

Centre Pompidou

PARIS, FRANCE

The Centre National d'Art et de Culture Georges Pompidou, known variously as the Pompidou and the Beaubourg, is one of the most hotly debated works of the last century, but it is also one of the world's most visited museums of modern art, welcoming up to 25,000 people a day. The Beaubourg is the seductive materialization of avant-garde dreams, a utopia come true that holds the provocative and transgressive drive of the futurist, surrealist and metabolist movements. The Beaubourg represents the synthesis of the crosscutting research of radical architects and artists at the height of the populist and revolutionary cultural turmoil prior to 1968. It unabashedly evokes Archigram's steel flying machines, reinterprets the node points and three-

philosophy of the Beaubourg, designed by two budding young architects, barely in their thirties, who won an international competition to which over 600 architects submitted plans.

Renzo Piano and Richard Rogers took a straightforward approach to the competition requirements. The conventional type of museum was considered obsolete for the figurative expressions of the neo-avant-garde, the products of industrial design and music. In particular, it was unsuitable for transforming the art market into business. Consequently, it was essential to contemplate changeable exhibition rooms, large spaces, support areas for archives, storerooms, offices and libraries, and set up commercial areas ranging from retail bookshops to restaurants and information points.

dimensional frameworks of Buckminster Fuller, calls to mind the spaceships of science-fiction movies, and evokes the nuclear power plants of the Cold War that, in the early Seventies when the museum was designed to be built in the historic center of Paris, was foremost in people's minds. But the Beaubourg is a *wunderkammer*, the venue of memorable exhibitions that attracted records crowds: in 1980 the anthological exhibition on Salvador Dalí drew 840,000 visitors, and the *Paris-Moscow* show nearly 430,000. These figures express the concept and

Everything was concentrated in a container that Piano and Rogers modeled in a tangle of steel pipes and color-coded ducts. The composition and layout are extremely simple and were designed to forge a connection with the surrounding area. Five overlaid rectangular plates – each of which 165 feet deep, 557 long and 23 high, and completely disjointed from the perimeter structure – create vast and functional open spaces. Like the empty volumes of a cathedral, the plan of these extended platforms ensures an extraordinarily flexible layout.

Centre Pompidou

Depending on the themes and size of the works being displayed, partitions can be set up to meet exhibition needs, permitting countless configurations.

This first design choice provides key insight into the Beaubourg, going beyond its high-tech aspect and the enormous impact of its image on the city: the museum was designed to take on a clearly urban character. Its volume is set along one side of the building lot, creating a plaza that is the fulcrum of the project. It serves as a second plein-air museum for street artists who have not discovered glory within the walls of institutions, but it is also a place where tourists can meet and relax.

This outside space flows into the ground floor, which is effectively the covered extension of the public square. The escalator visible on the main façade, the terrace/belvederes on the upper floors and the panoramic restaurant afford uncommon views of the mansard roofs of Paris, creating an exceptional and seamless connection between the building and the city, metaphorically interpenetrated by a solid and intentional rapport.

The importance acquired by the traditional urban elements of the city that have been conveyed inside the building compels us to observe the Beaubourg from a viewpoint that is less influenced by its unmistakable futurist thrust, grounding it in reality and garnering the public acclaim that has made the Paris museum an icon of contemporaneity.

Indeed, it is effectively a "vertical city" complete with plazas, concourses, and galleries to which two other separate departments – also designed by Piano – were later added: the IRCAM music center and the studio of the sculptor Costantin Brancusi, reconstructed in an annexed stone pavilion. This critical reevaluation towards the hyperbole expressed by its image was suggested by its very construction process, akin to the fine-tuning of a prototype and thus inspired by rules and craftsmanship.

Centre Pompidou

The framework of the Beaubourg is governed by the modularity of the parts that were used. The bearing system of the welded structure is composed of enormous lattice girders and piers that form the bays of the three-part elevation, and it is reinforced by the tie rods of the façades, which are glazed with full-length panels to illuminate the interior. The factory-cast elements were transported and assembled on site in a matter of hours, in a simplified management process using standardized parts.

This concept was also extended to the escalators and the prefabricated "capsules" with the bathrooms, which can theoretically be dismantled and readapted anywhere else in the museum to cater to current needs.

The structural framework is anchored to the visible network of ducts extending horizontally along the roof and ground, embellishing the rear elevation. Blue is used for the air ducts, green for water pipes, yellow for electrical cables and red for circulation: these elements are grouped together and clearly flaunt their presence.

The third construction system is composed of the lightweight bolted structures of the walkways, grid railings, and metal fittings anchored to the primary system. Through this

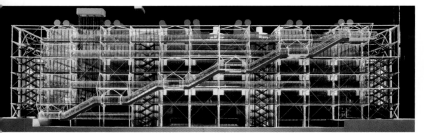

simplified reduction of the construction process, the Beaubourg overtly distances itself from the complexity typical of high-tech architecture, of which it is mistakenly considered the primary manifesto. The astonishing influx of over 150 million visitors to the Beaubourg in its first 20 years made it necessary to reorganize its layout, which had already been altered with respect to the original through Gae Aulenti's work in the Eighties. The museum was thus closed for renovation and reopened on January 1, 2000, symbolically inaugurating the new millennium.

With plans by Piano, 86,000 square feet were added to the 1 million square feet of exhibition space. The administrative offices were moved to an adjacent building, creating a separate entrance for the library, which was expanded to improve access to the new book collections that have been acquired. Changes were also made to the forum on the ground floor, using mezzanines for eateries and shops, and installing zoomorphic metal elements by Jakob & McFarlane in the panoramic restaurant on the rooftop of the Beaubourg. (Matteo Agnoletto)

46 and 46-47 The final version
of the model against a dark
background, and a night view of
the Centre Pompidou
demonstrate the building's
significant rapport with the night

in an area like Beaubourg that
attracts thousands of tourists 24
hours a day. The restoration work
done on the museum in the late
Nineties paid special attention to
lighting, creating color effects

that enhance its function as a
container for modern and
contemporary art. On the right, a
close-up of the square and the air
vents, which Umberto Eco dubbed
"the ears of hell."

48 and 49 top The long line of clear escalators connects earth and sky. From the square, visitors can climb to the panoramic rooftop terraces without ever entering the museum.

49 center and bottom As shown in the construction drawings, the escalator hugs the building and is completely separate from the bearing structure of the museum. Therefore, during the planning phase it was designed as a very

light and transparent element. The same circular cross section was also repeated in the external covered corridors leading to the various exhibition floors, applying a uniform and modular concept for the transit areas.

Centre Pompidou

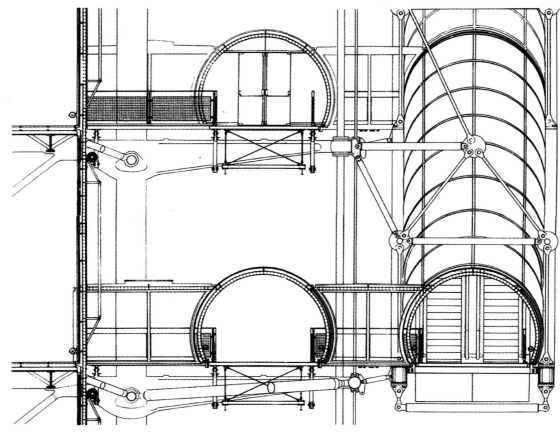

50-51 Due to the enormous influx of visitors – the average is 25,000 people a day, as opposed to the expected figure of 15,000 – the Centre Pompidou was closed to the public in the late Nineties to be restored. The interior was renovated on a functional level, updating its interior design and visual communications based on new plans. This redevelopment work allowed Piano to upgrade the entrances and add other public areas to support the exhibition areas. A staircase in the middle of the entrance forum goes down to the mezzanine; the café level is visible on the right.

51 With respect to the original plans, the new image of the Centre Pompidou is enhanced by color and by the lighting system, designed by IGuzzini.
A close-up of the exhibition space shows the new partition walls. The dual level of the ground floor and basement opens onto the pedestrian plaza with a glass wall.

Centre Pompidou

52-53 and 53 top The concept of the five overlaid open spaces – floors that are completely open to house temporary exhibitions and permanent collections – ensures optimum flexibility. This allows the museum to host contemporary art events and performances, which often require enormous spaces to accommodate large works. The individual floors, which are 23 feet tall, measure 164 by 558 feet, forming areas for exhibitions that are set up differently according to themes and topics.

53 center and bottom The rooms are closed at the top by girders that are 42 feet apart and weigh 132 tons each. The equipment ducts are installed in the hollow spaces. This "technological ceiling" is contrasted by a space finished with white plasterboard walls and new wooden floors, bounded by glass walls that allow visitors to admire the art inside the museum as well as the Parisian architecture outside.

Centre Pompidou

Institut du Monde Arabe

PARIS, FRANCE

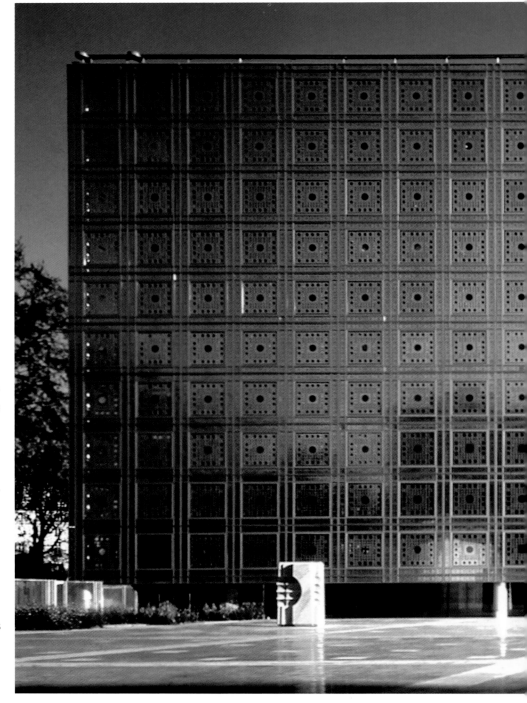

54-55 A series of Moorish decorative motifs reveals a combination of modern materials and patterns: the cladding panels are actually diaphragms like the ones inside cameras.

The Institut du Monde Arabe (IMA, or Arab World Institute), designed by the French architect Jean Nouvel and built between 1981 and 1987, is situated in Paris at the corner of Quai Saint-Bernard, near the university campus at Jussieu. It is wedged between the historic district of the French capital and the city's area of expansion to the southeast.

Part of Mitterand's *Les Grands Projets* program, it was conceived, designed, and built to accomplish the fascinating mission of representing France's relationship with the Arab civilization and culture.

From a city-planning standpoint, the architect's concept proposed a building that, on the north side, would follow the slight bend in the Seine and jut into the traditional urban fabric. The building towards the university is situated on a large square that separates it and cleverly creates a proportional relationship with the buildings of the academic institute.

The building is a multipurpose area, housing a library with thousands of books, a museum on Arab art and civilization from the 8th century to the contemporary era, a mediatheque, a theater, an auditorium, a bookshop and, on the 9th floor, a restaurant with a spectacular view of the Seine and the city's historic monuments. Visitors enter the IMA through a "cleft" opened on the west side towards the square patio. This patio is the true heart of the building, offering intense, shimmering vistas and imparting a sensation of spatial expansion. In essence, it is reminiscent of the Moorish tradition of courtyard houses.

The west end resembles an enormous white marble sculpture with a spiral shape that formally takes up the stylistic elements of the minarets of ancient mosques and houses the book tower, enclosed in a clear shell.

But the building's powerful formal expression is constituted by the south façade. Its composition represents the exemplary solution of the desired relationship between the Arab culture and modernity by reinterpreting what, from afar, resembles a series of Moorish motifs. Upon closer examination, however, it is actually a combination of historic references created with modern materials and patterns, in the form of diaphragms like the ones on cameras.

The designer keenly grasped the need to express the instrumental predominance of these transparent elements with respect to their formal qualities: the correct, variable and "intelligent" modulation of light entering the building. This has been achieved using over 30,000 panes of photosensitive glass, set in a structure with 240 steel aperture diaphragms sandwiched between two panes of protective glass to form square panels (6 x 6'). Each one can be opened or closed by a variable transmission percentage, and they are controlled by photocells and regulated through a computerized system.

The halls inside the building take up the same interplay of spatial expansion-contraction found in the city-planning solution, and one clearly detects the intention of proposing – but with a modern slant – a close parallel with Arabic installations. The French architect justified his design choices as "a matter of good manners," explaining that the reference to a Moorish courtyard enhances the setting for Arab art so it will not be viewed in rooms whose form is alien to these works. (Francesco Boccia)

DESIGN	CONSTRUCTION	DIMENSIONS	USE
J. Nouvel	1981-1987	Total area 272,237 square ft	Cultural center, library, museum of Arab art and civilization, mediatheque, auditorium, bookshop, restaurant

55 bottom A longitudinal section of the building: the central patio – the heart of the structure – is characterized by ever-changing reflections of light, and it visibly evokes the construction system of traditional Moorish courtyard houses. The floors at the Institut du Monde Arabe house various functions, such as a library, a museum, and a restaurant.

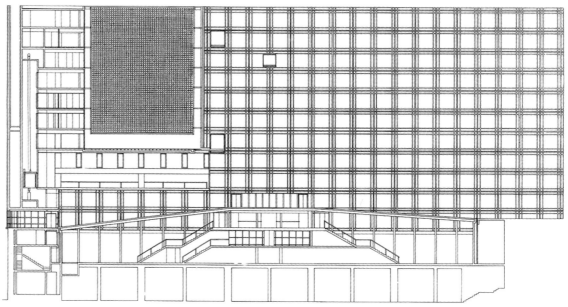

57 bottom left The interplay of light is a predominant element of the Institut du Monde Arabe in Paris. According to Nouvel, it is a Western building that acquires symbolic value in relation to the Arab culture.

57 bottom right From a city-planning standpoint, the Institute connects two areas that arose in different periods: the diaphragms of the south façade face modern Paris with a contemporary Eastern expression; on the north side, historic Paris is mirrored in the glass wall that follows the bend in the Seine.

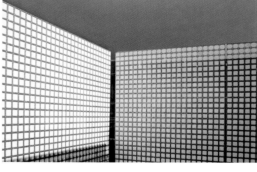

56-57 and 57 top The representatives of the 19 Arab countries that commissioned the project were extremely surprised by Jean Nouvel's proposal.

57 center The Institut du Monde Arabe (IMA) or Arab World Institute, designed by Jean Nouvel and built between 1981 and 1987, is wedged between one of the historic districts and the city's area of expansion.

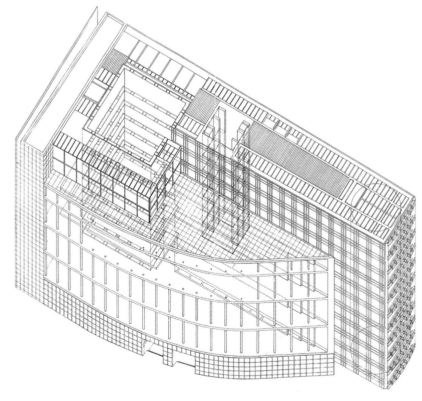

Institut du Monde Arabe

58-59 This exhibition room illustrates the play of light created by the Institut du Monde Arab's 30,000 panels of photosensitive glass that compose the 240 panels holding the diaphragms.

59 top The unique definition of space makes the building a distinctive multipurpose venue as an exhibition area but, even more importantly, as a cultural center and place to socialize that is open to the city.

59 center The formal allusion to the arrangement of construction elements and spatial patterns typical of Arab architecture are a point of contact that the French architect has reinterpreted simply but meticulously.

59 bottom According to Nouvel, the design choices pinpointed as essential for this building are "a matter of good manners" intended to create the best setting to display the works.

Institut du Monde Arabe

Institut du Monde Arabe

60 The unit with the stairs and elevators introduces an element typical of modernity to a building that endlessly evokes the Moorish tradition: the transparency and evanescence of glass, supported by a metal structure that breaks with tradition and represents technological innovation.

61 The book tower, enclosed in an enormous clear glass shell, is at the west end of the building. The architect conceived of the tower as a white marble sculpture, and the resulting design – a spiral shape – evokes the stylistic elements of the minarets of ancient mosques.

62-63 The glass pyramid is the linchpin of the new Louvre. Fountains and pools, and smaller pyramids that serve as skylights, complete the courtyard. This work dialogues with ancient structures through allusions to traditional historical forms and the parallels between the materials that were used.

63 top Maintenance workers scale the sloped surfaces of the Louvre Pyramid to clean and polish the glass – an endless task.

DESIGN	CONSTRUCTION	DIMENSIONS	USE
I.M. PEI	1983-1989	TOTAL AREA 13,487 SQUARE FT	ART MUSEUM

The Louvre Pyramid

PARIS, FRANCE

The European city poised on the threshold of the third millennium has been marked by several inevitable transformations. As part of this change, the museum has taken on a leading role. New structures have been built, bringing uncommon visibility and fame to marginal cities, such as Bilbao with the construction of the Guggenheim Museum and Manchester with the War Museum. Other Western capitals have recovered important derelict areas, the most notable example of which is the conversion of an abandoned factory in London into the Tate Modern. Barcelona, followed by Rome, opted for ultramodern museums erected in the ancient heart of their urban fabric and designed by luminaries such as Richard Meier and Zaha Hadid. The example set by Paris was the harbinger of these strategic choices, as it was the first to view museums as sites for the urban and economic redevelopment of a city. The policies enacted by François Mitterand in the early Eighties focused entirely on valorizing institutions, and particularly national public museums. The transformation of the Orsay Train Station into exhibition space and the decision to turn the entire Louvre into a museum gave Paris' cultural and artistic circuit important hubs devoted to highly prestigious artwork. The Ministry of Finance was moved to other premises, freeing the Richelieu wing of the Louvre on the Rue de Rivoli side. This made it possible to expand the royal palace, which had radically been modified during the Baroque period by the court architect Claude Perrault, and was later remodeled for other uses during the reigns of Louis XIV and Napoleon Bonaparte. Because of the need to accommodate the museum's extraordinary collections and attract more visitors, project development focused on expanding the exhibition rooms. The unequivocal goal of this project was to create the Grand Louvre, conceived of as a "total museum" for painting and sculpture, and home to Leonardo da Vinci's Mona Lisa and the Venus de Milo. Government authorities unexpectedly awarded the commission directly to I.M. Pei, attracting much criticism. The Chinese-American architect had designed the East Wing of the National Gallery of Art in Washington D.C., for which he won the 1983 Pritzker Price, the sought-after award that, among architects, is the equivalent of a Nobel Prize. Excavation operations and

63 center To establish the size of the Louvre Pyramid in relation to the monumental façades around it, following Madame Pompidou's indications a 1:1 scale model was built to demonstrate the impact that the project – greatly criticized when it was presented – would have on the surrounding architecture. After this experiment, Mitterand decided to approve the plans to build the pyramid.

63 bottom The Baroque elements of the Louvre Palace dialogue with the transparency of the glass pyramid, creating a harmonious rapport between ancient and modern.

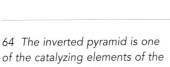
The Louvre Pyramid

64 The inverted pyramid is one of the catalyzing elements of the underground mall. It serves two important purposes: it is an enormous skylight that lets in natural light to illuminate the long foyer and museum halls, but it is also a symbolic element. The sophisticated concept of poising the tip of the glass pyramid so that it almost touches a smaller pyramid – a stone sculpture rising from the floor – evokes Michelangelo's famous painting in the Sistine Chapel, portraying God's finger outstretched towards Adam's.

65 A steel spiral staircase leads from the courtyard to the interior of the museum. The photograph illustrates the structure and the Louvre Palace.

work to upgrade the historic buildings began in 1984. Pei's enormous addition was already open to the public by 1989, and work on the Richelieu wing was completed in 1993. Pei's design immediately raised a number of fundamental issues: the Louvre needed a new and representative access for the public, and a different functional organization by rerouting tour itineraries. In order to avoid constructing a new building next to the Louvre, the service and reception areas were created underground. The Cour Napoléon, the paved courtyard set at the intersection of the east-west and north-south lines of the palace, was selected as the entrance to the crypts.

The entrance is surmounted by the famous shimmering glass pyramid, which closes the visual perspective uniting the architecture of the Louvre with the geometric Tuileries Gardens, designed Le Nôtre during the late Renaissance. Pei actually set four glass pyramids in the middle of the square. The main one, which is 69 feet tall and 108 wide, serves as both an entryway and a roof over the winding steel staircase that leads to the museum's underground hall. The staircase clearly alludes to the

spiral staircase in reinforced concrete that Le Corbusier built in the 1930s at Ville Savoye, on the outskirts of Paris.

The other pyramids, which are smaller, are skylights for the spaces beneath. Pei offset the stone and stuccowork of the monumental façades of the French palace with the brilliance and gleam of steel and glass, which was made using ultra-fine sand from Fontainbleau; he brought in the modern technology of metal cable structures, and the mechanized systems of escalators and round elevators. This design concept culminates with the predominant form of the pyramid, the oldest archetype of the stylistic elements with which his structure must dialogue. The pools and fountains around it multiply the reflection of light, projecting evanescent shafts of silver onto the pedestrian areas around the Pyramid. The underground platform has a tunnel illuminated by a fifth overturned pyramid, the *pyramide inversée*, which captures natural light from the outside and conveys it into the transit areas. This creates an invisible connection with the surface, linking the older wings of the

I.M. PEI

palace with Pei's addition. The new section includes an auditorium, restoration workshops, restaurants, boutiques and offices, and extends to the parking areas under the Carrousel Gardens and the subway station. Boldly representing the contemporary age, the translucent image of Pei's glass walls add another linguistic layer to the historic and architectural legacy of the Louvre, which dates back to the 13th Century, and the construction of Philip Augustus' fortress, which was later transformed into a royal residence by Charles V. As visitors cross the square with the Pyramid or look up from the new atrium of the museum, they are greeted by the sloped surfaces of the Pyramid, which capture the ancient palace in all its stately splendor. The central position of this icon accentuates its symbolic meaning: Pei made the new entrance equidistant from the three wings of the palace. As a result, it serves as a linchpin for all the buildings of the Louvre, shortening the paths between the different parts.

Because it expresses both the absence and presence of

contemporaneity in the face of history, and interprets the void of the courtyard and its concept of enclosed space, this center – intentionally dematerialized through the use of glass – has been analyzed in a number of ways. The complexity of the structural web of the pyramid, which holds 800 glass rhomboids, boasts state-of-the-art technology, making it one of the most sophisticated high-tech works to date. Its assembly process of beams, tie rods and node points was modeled by applying the extraordinarily precise techniques used for the sailboats that compete in the America's Cup. And yet the choice of the pyramid also makes Pei's Louvre the swansong of postmodernism. The very year it was inaugurated, on the other side of the world the Museum of Modern Art in New York opened its exhibition on architectural deconstructionism, the logical outcome of the classical linguistic assumptions that predominated in the Eighties – but the absolute negation of the regularity of form and the strict principles handed down over the course of history. (Matteo Agnoletto)

The Louvre Pyramid

Le Grand Arche de la Fraternité

PARIS, FRANCE

If there is an architectural work that succeeds in celebrating the grandeur of a city and country with spectacular power, it is the Grande Arche de la Fraternité in the La Défense district in Paris.

A splendid model of monumental architecture, it is the very essence and completion of the perspective sequence stretching from the Louvre up the Champs-Elysées to the Arche de Triomphe, and down to La Défense. The structure, designed by the Danish architect Johann Otto von Spreckelsen,

Arche de Triomphe at Place de l'Étoile. Unlike its illustrious predecessor, however, this work was dedicated to humanity rather than military victories.

The Grande Arche is almost a perfect cube, and the differences in its dimensions are barely noticeable, as it is 368 feet tall, 367.5 wide and 354 deep. Mere description conveys the grandeur of this structure: its roof weighs over 33,000 tons and has a surface of nearly 2.5 acres. Its façades are clad with more than 215,000 square feet of white Carrara marble and

demonstrates the extent to which a stark and simple form can be used express lines and surfaces that are taut and compelling, yet also light and ethereal, conveying a message of fluidity and compositional power destined to endure the centuries.

The Grande Arche was part of the *Grand Travaux*, an immense program in which 15 billion francs were invested to give France a series of monuments that would honor the country's central role in art, politics, and the world economy. The plans for the Arche de la Défense were inspired by the

269,000 square feet of glass. The entire building weighs more than 330,000 tons and is mounted on 12 pillars with hydraulic jacks, and it has more than 1 million square feet of office space on 35 floors.

With respect to the axis linking the Louvre and Place de l'Étoile the building is rotated about 6° off center. Though this was done for technical reasons, to ensure clearance for the highways and railroad lines, it also establishes symbolic continuity with the past and the historical city, as the angle of

68 top The façades are clad with 269,000 square feet of glass and more than 215,000 square feet of white Carrara marble.

DESIGN	CONSTRUCTION	DIMENSIONS	USE
O. VON SPRECKELSEN	1983-1989	TOTAL AREA 1,022,571 SQUARE FT	PUBLIC AND PRIVATE OFFICES

68 bottom The district of La Défense was named after the monument known as La Défense de Paris, erected here in 1883.

68-69 This view highlights the insertion of two formal elements in the void of the arch: the elevator block enclosed by metal latticework and the Nuage, a fiberglass-covered pavilion sustained by a tensile structure made of steel wires. The pavilion was designed by Paul Andreu, who completed the Grande Arche following the death of its architect.

69 bottom The Ésplanade de la Défense offers a stunning architectural perspective that conceptually concludes a series of monuments that starts with the Louvre. Over half a mile long, the Ésplanade is open only to pedestrians, and it boasts artwork as well as public and private buildings completed between the late Fifties and the Nineties.

70 top *The interior of the Grande Arche de la Fraternité, hollowed out from an architectural sculpture that is virtually a perfect cube, is as wide as the Champs Elysées and is tall enough to hold Notre-Dame Cathedral.*

70 center *The framework supporting the roof of the two entrance lobbies creates a contrast with the façades of the Grande Arche: the former is small but highly complex, whereas the latter are linear and monumental.*

Le Grand Arche de la Fraternité

rotation is the same as one between the central axis and the position of the Louvre.

The bold symbol of the deep-rooted sense of grandeur of the French, the Grande Arche was inaugurated in 1989 to celebrate the bicentennial of the French Revolution and the Declaration of the Rights of Man. This massive cube is presented as pure and extreme form, making no concessions to forced proportional relations with the exterior. It expresses sculptural quality on an uncommon scale – even within the magnificent setting of the Ésplanade, the extraordinary pedestrian prospect boasting artwork and buildings completed between the late Fifties and the Nineties. François Mitterand chose Von Spreckelsen's project from the 420 that were submitted to the *Tête Défense* competition from around the world, defining it as "noteworthy because of its purity and the power with which it creates a new point of reference along the *Axe historique* of Paris." Construction work began in 1983 and was handled by the French civil engineering company Bouygues. The north and south parts of the building house government offices, whereas the upper part of the Grande Arche is occupied by a congress and exhibition center, which has a rooftop terrace. The terrace, which is open to the public, can be accessed using the panoramic elevator. The Danish architect died in 1987, before the Grande Arche was opened, and the architect Paul Andreu completed the work. (Francesco Boccia)

70 bottom *The view from the interior of one of the two entrances to the vertical parts of the Grande Arche highlights the expressive divergence between the roof of the Nuage pavilion and the rest of the structure of this Paris monument.*

71 *The design concept of the Danish architect Johann Otto von Spreckelsen is oriented towards the seamless modularity of the internal and external partitions, in order to respond to functional and compositional needs.*

The National Library

PARIS, FRANCE

The Bibliothèque Nationale de France – the National Library of France – was constructed following an architectural design competition held by the French government in 1989 to build the world's largest library. Promoted by President François Mitterand during his second seven-year term of office as part of the sweeping *Grands Travaux* program, the library was part of the urban development project undertaken in Paris in the Eighties and Nineties, and it reflects the philosophy and spirit of the era.

In Mitterand's political program, Paris was to be transformed into a city of museums and culture, dotted with ambitious modern monuments: Parc de la Villette, the Cité de la Musique, the Grande Arche de la Défense, the Louvre Pyramid and the Opéra de la Bastille. As part of this new generation of architecture, Dominique Perrault's Library holds dual significance. One is institutional, representing the knowledge collected in books and democratically available to all. At the same time,

however, it is a center that revitalizes the urban landscape of a specific part of the city. The National Library is situated in Tolbiac, in the 13ème Arrondissement on the left bank of the Seine. It is composed of a vertical system represented by four glass towers, designed to evoke an open book, that are set at the corners of an elevated rectangular platform. In the center, a garden brings light and greenery into the reception and reading areas created in the massive horizontal stone base. Those using the different rooms are completely isolated from the street and the outside environment, and are surrounded by the wisdom emanated by books, amidst leafy trees and light that streams in overhead. As a result, the public space is introverted and overlooks the garden. Instead, the vertical glass prisms of the Library, new elements in the cityscape, are not open to readers and are designed exclusively to contain books.

The message here is clearly symbolic: the invincibility of the towers expresses the accumulation of man's indestructible

72 The interior faces of the library are designed as public meeting areas. The balconies, made of wood and metal, punctuate the corridors to diminish the monumental effect of the height of the building. Outside, the staircase leading to the elevated square separates the towers from the street: the distinction between the horizontal platform of the stone base and the vertical development of the glass towers is also emphasized by the use of different materials.

72-73 The façade of the towers is composed of a double skin that is completely closed and has no windows: the outer layer is made of glass, whereas opaque panels ensure that no light can enter.

DESIGN	CONSTRUCTION	DIMENSIONS	USE
D. PERRAULT	1992-1995	TOTAL AREA 3,930,743 SQUARE FT	LIBRARY

73 bottom The towers are set at the four corners of the central garden that "pierces" the base of the elevated square. Arranged to resemble an open book, they frame the view of the city of Paris.

74-75 The complex of the four library towers plays an important role in the urban landscape of this part of Paris. Because of its setting in relation to the Seine and the use of evocative nocturnal lighting, the complex can easily be recognized even from a distance.

74 bottom These views demonstrate Perrault's minimalist attention in the treatment of space, using detailing as an organizing symbol. The internal perspective lines of the long corridors, the use of trees and plants, and the open workspace were designed to cater to the crowds of people who use the library every day.

75 The furnishings in the reading rooms, the choice of colors and materials, and meticulous research into artificial lighting proved to be decisive in terms of the general outcome of the building. The library areas thus gain a specific identity based on the order and geometric uniformity of the parts.

knowledge. Visible from afar – they can be seen from many parts of Paris – they evoke the role of the ancient spires of Gothic cathedrals. Like the pinnacles crowning Parisian churches, the towers have become inimitable elements of the cityscape.

The magic of the National Library is evident in the layout of its labyrinthine interior. Leaving the city streets behind, one climbs the monumental staircase to the hanging plaza that affords a view of the rooftops of Paris from an uncommon vantage point. From this immense void isolated from chaos and city traffic – a void that prepares the visitor for the concentration of reading – one descends into the library's secret chambers via the escalator in the garden.

The woods Perrault created in the heart of his building herald the peaceful stillness of the reading rooms. The visitor enters enormous rooms finished in natural materials: glass, wood, and the natural fabrics used for the draperies and upholstery. Research and consultation areas, restoration workshops, audiovisual archives and recordings, and an advanced circulation system make the use and operation of the National Library extremely innovative. It is an architecture that involuntarily overturns Victor Hugo's harsh words: *ceci tuera cela*. Books do not destroy architecture. and, indeed, it is architecture that holds and preserves them forever.
(Matteo Agnoletto)

76 top The enormous roof wing of the main concourse of the terminal is a distinctive element of the city of Lyon and a tribute to modern means of transportation.

76 bottom The white concrete support structures serve as zoomorphic skeletons, representing the sculptural expressiveness that has become Calatrava's hallmark.

The TGV Station
LYON, FRANCE

In 1994 an enormous white bird landed at Lyon-Saint Exupéry Airport in France: the new TGV station, designed by the Spanish architect Santiago Calatrava, linking the airport to the city. Calatrava won an international competition (called by the Rhône-Alpes Regional Council) whose objective was to create a monument symbolizing the region, and a powerful sign generated by the station's architectural structure that would be instantly recognizable to those approaching it, whether by land or air.

Train and plane have been reconciled here, as the axis of the runways matches the linearity of the tracks. Their coexistence is underscored by the impressive structure enclosing the main hall: an enormous overturned V made of reinforced concrete, dominated by vast steel wings outstretched so that their technological performance can protect the curvature of the long vaults covering the platforms, the unmistakable sign that there are trains here.

The plans use a simple layout composed of two main bodies set at a right angle. One is the building for travelers, occupied mainly by the large arrivals and departures hall; the other is the roofing vault composed of a diagonal bracing structure with white concrete girders and lozenge-shaped skylights. The roofing, 184 feet wide and nearly 1500 feet long, covers the six tracks and the passenger concourse. The enormous hall dominates the infrastructure of the tracks and

walkways, and is laid out crosswise with respect to the roofing vault, dividing it into two symmetrical parts. The central hall is triangular and the different passenger routes extend from here. The main access is connected to the service area (with shops, five restaurants, two hotels, meeting rooms and a space for temporary exhibitions) and the airport check-in desks, channeling the flow of passengers towards the long transversal concourse. Two enormous steel arches rise from the vertex of the triangle in front of the entrance and extend to the other two vertices on the opposite side, defining the north and south faces. Above the arches, laid out to form a triangle, there is another structure made of steel-and-glass sections that can be swiveled to increase ventilation in the hall.

From the main hall, the transit area to the airport can be accessed via two escalators that lead to two impressive cantilevered balconies. The roofing over the train area forms a multilevel gallery. The tracks and platforms are on the lower floor, 26 feet below ground level. The central part is comprised of an enclosed area, through which the TGV trains transit at nearly 190 mph without stopping. The slab over this central area forms the upper gallery, connected to the platforms by stairs and escalators. From this walkway and rest area, visitors can watch moving trains and observe crowds on the lower level.

These areas and spaces are strictly defined in terms of their functional characteristics and type, evoking the models of the most important train stations of the late 19th century. Nevertheless, in the meticulous design of the bearing structure Calatrava plies his artistic insight and expressionist language to make visible the dynamism of the forces at play, bearing witness to the fundamental role of railways as swift, modern means of transportation. This is a simple and readily understandable structure that evokes flight, a sculpture in which the architect's expressiveness is entrusted to the plasticity of the structures.

Tellingly, Calatrava was a sculptor before he turned to architecture. He attended art school in Valencia, his native city, and has long been aware of the interdependency

76-77 The two simple intersecting volumes generate spaces typical of 19th-century stations. In this case, the work takes on poetic value, representing the perfect union of aesthetics and function. This effect is achieved through painstaking design and control over the lines of force that come into play in the dynamism of this structure.

77 bottom The roofing over the train platforms is nearly 1500 feet long. The terminal represented a brand-new concept when the competition to award this project was held, as it involved Europe's first modern intermodal hub.

DESIGN	CONSTRUCTION	DIMENSIONS	USE
S. CALATRAVA	1989-1994	TOTAL AREA 269,098 SQUARE FT	HIGH-SPEED TRAIN INTERCHANGE STATION

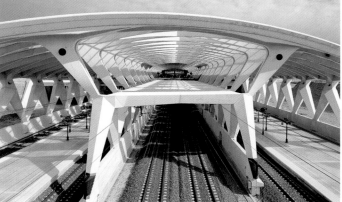

The TGV Station

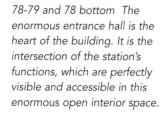

78-79 and 78 bottom The enormous entrance hall is the heart of the building. It is the intersection of the station's functions, which are perfectly visible and accessible in this enormous open interior space.

From here, visitors can take a moving sidewalk to get to the airport 650 feet away. The station services can be accessed via walkways and escalators that lead to the upper level or down to the train platforms.

79 The even geometric arrangement of the ribbing of the passenger concourse evokes the enormous belly of a white concrete whale that is aligned with the airport runways.

between sculpture and architecture. Here we find the motif of a sculpture created by the architect, similar to the shell of the airport he designed at Bilbao, which emerges from the ground to rise into the air. At the TGV station, it is a moving sphere beneath a sheet of metal that has been bent to form two wings poised in flight: the abstract icon of flying that conveys the powerful symbolism of the balance of natural forces.

It is common to compare the great architects-engineers in the history of architecture, and in Calatrava's sculptural approach we can perceive the differences between his expressions and those of Pier Luigi Nervi and Riccardo Morandi. The principle behind traditional engineering is that

form is the highest sublimation of calculation, the point of arrival of a mathematical and scientific formulation. In Calatrava's case, calculation and technical know-how are the tools and investigative approaches employed to achieve form. On the one hand, we have research into the richest spatial solution among the many that are technically equivalent, and on the other we have technology and engineering that – in the architect's words – represent "the art of the possible." This statement is backed by the value of expressive research, which is thrust into the field of abstraction and dynamic equilibriums to be transformed from the art of rationality into the art of possibility.

Calatrava's artistic approach to architectural design is

The TGV Station

80-81 and 80 bottom Though they are immobile, Calatrava's signature works always suggest the idea of motion and mobility. In Lyon, this inspiring principle takes the form of a bird poised in flight.

81 The theme of light predominates inside the building. It filters through the laminated glass panels in the atrium and the concourses, entering this space laterally and from overhead to reveal the repetitive and

powerfully abstract rhythm of the structural forms. The enormous central vertebra of the hall supports over 1300 tons of steel, used to form the roofing wings and calculated to withstand 24 different types of loads.

further emphasized by the use and intrinsic properties of his materials: concrete and steel painted white, a disguise that eliminates their reciprocal differences. Whereas the Modern Movement strived to visually reveal the countless differences of the architectural object, expressing each material solely through its essence, Calatrava effectively forgoes the opportunity to establish a relationship between the observer of his architectures and the tactile, textural qualities of these works. He thus excludes the observer from the work's developmental process, the stratified event in which each transition is the result of manifold factors and decisions related to context and the community as a whole.

By rejecting tangible stratification, the "skin" of his edifices, he brings out their expressive power, contributing to his primary design objective: focusing the eyes and heart of

the observer on the complex spatial image that originates from the small-scale circumstances of everyday spatial experiences. Their singularity often stems from the fact that they are not bound to their surroundings, though their design tends to evoke the natural elements around them. For example, the curve of a bridge calls to mind the outline of the nearby hills; a roof in the shape of a wave echoes the sea visible just beyond. But their involvement ends here. As Calatrava himself declares, his buildings are "autonomous." They are individual events that occupy their assigned territory, augmenting the order and control they hold over it based on the tenet that "the universe works according to a predetermined geometric model." Nothing is random, and his architectures clearly aspire to affirm this principle. (Marco Tagliatori)

82-83 Designed for an invited competition held in 1956, the new hall for the Berlin Philharmonic Orchestra replaced the building on Bernburgerstrasse, which was destroyed by Allied bombs in 1944. The Berlin State Library, also designed by Scharoun, was built next to it in 1964.

82 bottom In 1959, the decision to move the new building from Bundesallee to Kemperplatz at the Tiergarten did not change the architect's original plans. Extensions were added, mainly for equipment and service facilities for the Philharmonie.

DESIGN	CONSTRUCTION	DIMENSION	USE
H. SCHAROUN	1961-1963	VOLUME 141,259 CUBIC YARDS	AUDITORIUM

The Philharmonie

During the culturally vibrant 1920s, Hans Scharoun stood out for his critical approach to rationalism, sustaining the emotional aspect stirred by the architectural manipulation of space, in marked opposition to the impermeability of the binomial of form and function.

The first part of his career as an architect is an example of his adherence to this conviction, as demonstrated by his masterpiece from this period, the Schminke House in Löbau (1933). This building does not disdain the geometric lines that, according to his contemporary Hugo Häring, were the death of vital energy. Yet by twisting, dilating, and compressing the body of this structure, Scharoun shunned the immobility of the rigid, boxy vision that was becoming rampant during this period and that would later explosively emerge in some of the eyesores of postwar reconstruction.

Indeed, World War II was a watershed in Scharoun's life. Following the Nazi rise to power, the architect was virtually forced underground, and he designed extensively during this long period of self-imposed isolation. Though he was physically confined, his mind was free to roam, exploring the utopian architecture of Bruno Taut, and the formal freedom of Häring and Hermann Finsterlin, and imaging democratic spaces in which the urban scale merges with the very structure of buildings.

Scharoun thus entered his full artistic maturity when, backed by his enormous experience and powerful personality, he approached the most extremist concepts of the architectural expressionism that was cut short by Hitler's madness. This was an extremely prolific period for him, with notable works such as the Geschwister Scholl High School in Lünen, the Romeo and Juliet apartment building in Stuttgart, and the Berlin *Philharmonie* (Philharmonic Hall), when he won the 1956 competition for

83 bottom This building, which reflects Scharoun's full artistic maturity, takes up the most extreme concepts of the expressionist movement. These architectural activities came to a halt under Hitler, who forced many German architects – including Scharoun – to stop working or flee the country.

84-85 The architect's organic conception is evident in the shape of the roof, designed as an enormous sculptural tent made of ocher concrete. As Bruno Zevi noted, it "battles monumentality with a seemingly temporary shell," symbolizing the aggregation that takes place inside it.

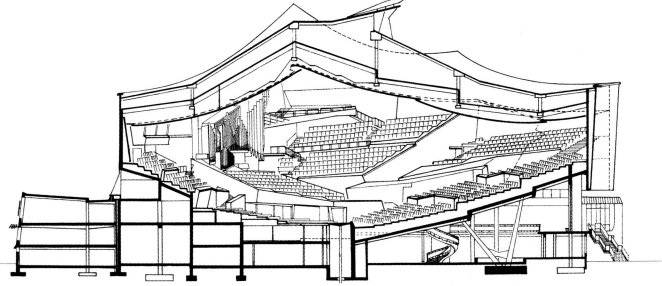

The Philharmonie

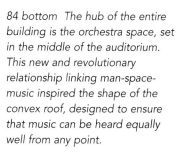

84 bottom The hub of the entire building is the orchestra space, set in the middle of the auditorium. This new and revolutionary relationship linking man-space-music inspired the shape of the convex roof, designed to ensure that music can be heard equally well from any point.

85 top and bottom right The hexagonal layout is perfectly symmetrical, with 2200 seats that encircle the space devoted to music. Observed from one of the sides, however, the auditorium reveals its full dynamism and spatial variety. Depending on

requirements, the orchestra stage can be lowered and narrowed to accommodate different types of performances. The blocks extending towards the orchestra break up the classic separation between the musicians and the audience.

85 bottom left The Kammermusiksaal, or chamber music hall, was designed by the architect Edgar Wisniewski, a pupil of Scharoun, and was built in 1987. Its construction completed the concept for the Kulturforum, which Scharoun had planned nearly 30 years earlier.

designing a new auditorium for the new concert hall. His plans, which were immediately praised by the conductor Herbert von Karajan, were profoundly innovative, starting with the decision to place the orchestra in the middle of the auditorium, not only to make music the fulcrum of the building, but also to create a sense of community with audiences. The desire for social unity is evident throughout the work, from the exterior of the building evoking the shape of circus tents to the extraordinary layout of the concert hall itself, designed to accommodate 2200 people at a maximum distance of 105 feet from the stage, in a seemingly random seating arrangement. The goal was to create the atmosphere of a group of enthusiasts gathered informally around a street performance. Each seating sector has independent access points that form a foyer with an array of ramps and routes staggered on

several levels, effectively forcing concert-goers to cross the building and take in ever-changing vistas. The roofing is one of the hallmarks of the building, but it was also designed to optimize acoustics, as sound is the direct medium between performers and audiences. At the same time, the container itself tends to dissolve to leave the impression of an impromptu gathering. A reflection of the German economic miracle, the Berlin Philharmonie was not built on the lot originally indicated in the competition but in an area of West Berlin near the Wall. This area became the location of the Staatsbibliothek (the German State Library), also designed by Scharoun, and Mies van der Rohe's Neue Nationalgalerie (New National Gallery), the emblem of "less is more" and the magnificent outcome of a diametrically opposed worldview. (Marco Tagliatori)

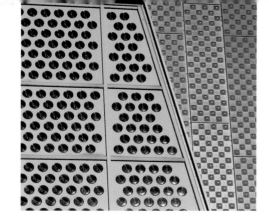

The Philharmonie

86-87 The main priority in Scharoun's plans involved acoustics, which were carefully researched. The sloped parapets have special resonators for low tones, the curvature of the false ceilings is designed to dispel sound instead of concentrating it in a specific direction, and the special protuberances from the ceiling reverberate low frequencies. The distinctive pattern of the ceiling creates the impression that music pours down from above, completely enveloping the listener.

87 top The exterior of Sharoun's masterful music hall was not completed until 1980 due to financial problems. Finally, the concrete surface was overlaid with polyester panels clad with gold-anodized aluminum.

87 center and bottom The shape of the concert hall also influences the layout of the foyer on the ground floor. Ramps and landings on different levels accompany concertgoers as they ascend, offering ever-changing vistas.

88-89 According to the definition of its architect, Daniel Libeskind, the new wing of the Berlin Museum represents the differences between two lines of thought, organization and relation: a straight one that is fragmented into various segments, and a winding but continuous one.

The Jewish Museum

BERLIN, GERMANY

Of the 165 proposals submitted for the design of the Jewish Museum in Berlin, the jury chose the one by the American architect Daniel Libeskind, considering it the most brilliant and complex.

Unlike the other plans that were presented, Libeskind's did not establish a proportional rapport between the nearby Kollegienhaus, the Baroque structure housing the Berlin Museum, and the new museum. Indeed, with over 80,000 square feet of exhibition space and 43,000 square feet for storerooms, offices, and the auditorium, the museum triples the space of the building on Lindenstrasse. His plans also stood out because of their intricate structure and form, composed a fractured and inclined organism with broken lines and uneven surfaces.

The museum is clad with a zinc-titanium alloy, a material used for the Kollegienhaus and common in Berlin's modern buildings. The color of the metal tends to turn greenish gray when exposed to the elements.

Inside, the structure spins out a path that crosses it, effectively serving as its backbone to represent the dawning awareness of a history that does not exist yet, but that we must begin to examine. The focal point of the museum is not its three-dimensional solidity but its absences, the voids between its walls. This concept establishes a new relationship between form and function, one that is no longer balanced and conventional but free and discontinuous. The entrance to the new museum is below the street level, and this is the starting point for the paths crisscrossing the complex.

The first one leads to the structure that has unofficially been named the Holocaust Tower, which is accessed from the basement level. This cavernous empty structure creates intriguing acoustics, echoing sound and conveying a sense of disorientation. The tower is an extraordinarily eloquent part of the museum in terms of its proportions, composition, and spatial relationships. The architect points out that this concrete structure is nameless because its subject is not the tactile part but the space within, illuminated by the natural light entering through a

89 top The idea of expanding the Berlin museum housed in the nearby Kollegienhaus stemmed from the desire of city planners to devote a new museum space to the Jewish community, as a tribute to its vital role in the history and culture of Berlin.

89 bottom Libeskind paralleled his intricate layout with equally complex elevations to create an alternation of solids and voids, yielding a segmented image with an intense and compelling form.

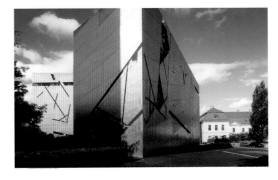

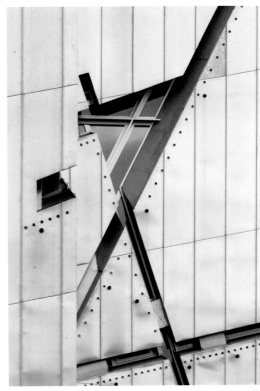

88 bottom The museum is clad with plates made of a zinc-titanium alloy, a material that is commonly seen in both old and new buildings in Berlin. The city and its Jewish community are symbolically linked by this choice of material and by the physical connection between the old building and the new museum.

DESIGN	CONSTRUCTION	DIMENSIONS	USE
D. LIBESKIND	1993-1999	TOTAL AREA 161,459 SQUARE FEET	JEWISH MUSEUM

90-91 The exterior walls of the structure are broken up by irregularly arranged windows of different shapes and sizes. This adds yet another element to the compositional language of the spatial, formal and functional layout of the spaces, and of the interior and exterior surfaces.

90 bottom Unlike the other architects who submitted plans to the design competition for the Jewish Museum, Libeskind did not attempt to forge a link between the new structure and the older one. Instead, he conceived of a completely new architectural body with an irregular layout, powerfully contrasting the existing urban lines.

The Jewish Museum

91 top Libeskind's museum gives architecture a clearly stabilizing function as part of an artificially arranged landscape, and it responds to the need to play a dual role, as a commemorative presence that looks back towards the past, but also as a first step in the city's future development.

91 bottom The angle of the outside walls, which resembles a bolt of lightning in the plan view, generates intermediate spaces in which perception is dramatically heightened. The façades, clad with zinc panels, create a sense of disorientation, as the Holocaust is described in an architectural form.

window that is barely perceptible from inside the tower.

The second path leads to the main transit area and the stairs. The windows reveal the street level, fragmented and uneven yet perceptible as a single stable horizon. The exhibition rooms are large and asymmetrical.

They are crossed by enclosed routes and sixty bridges that traverse the voids, connect the rooms, and generate an abstract and sculptural architecture, uniting line, space, and form to create an overpowering composition.

The exterior walls are broken up by irregularly arranged windows that make light yet another element in this complex.

The interior spaces are laid out like "unfinished" stories interrupted by small structures, with painted black screens that

The Jewish Museum

92 top Some of the bridges connecting the rooms can only be crossed visually.

92 center The rooms were conceived as unfinished stories, with windows that break up the walls to reveal the outside environment.

92 bottom According to Libeskind's description, the function of the paths inside is to interrupt the pace of the exhibitions in the museum, so that the walls – which are left bare and unused – are part of this narrative.

92-93 A long path crosses the rooms and represents their backbone, accompanying the exhibition structure and marking off the areas devoted to the exhibits. Every part of the museum was conceived as a tribute to the Jewish heritage and the culture of Berlin.

punctuate the narrative pace and introduce spatial, architectural, poetic and thematic distance. In the architect's conception, the paths complete the stories recounted by exhibitions. In turn, the exhibitions are interrupted by a path that crosses them, leaving walls unused, untouchable, and silent. These blank walls thus become an essential part of the exhibitions themselves, representing the human lives that will never have the chance to enter a museum. The path exiting the museum goes through the Garden of Exile and Emigration, with 49 concrete columns filled with earth. The columns, about five feet wide and 23 feet tall, are set about three feet apart; 48 of them – alluding to 1948, the year of Israel's independence – are filled with soil from Berlin, whereas one is filled with earth from Jerusalem. (Francesco Boccia)

The Reichstag

BERLIN, GERMANY

The original home of German democracy was seriously damaged by bombing during World War II and left in a rundown state until the 1960s, when it was insensitively renovated for use as a conference center. The most evident consequences of the work were the demolition of the dome and the lining of the historic interiors with plaster and asbestos panels.

When the Reichstag reverted to its role as home of the German Parliament in 1990, becoming the symbol of reunification, it was clear that the building needed to be adapted. In 1992, Foster's firm was one of fourteen 4 non-German practices invited to enter the competition to rebuild

the Reichstag. The practice won the competition after a second selection phase in 1993, and work began following Christo and Jeanne-Claude's *Wrapped Reichstag* project in 1995.

During demolition the structure of the old building was revealed, as were fragments of 19th-century molding, the imprints of the war, graffiti by Soviet soldiers, and the traces left by the builders during the work done in the Sixties.

It was decided not to delete all these traces of the past, but to preserve them and make them visible and distinguishable from each other, clearly illustrating the links between the different periods and the new work. This effectively makes the Reichstag a "living museum" of German history.

Foster himself has commented that the simplest

94 bottom and 95 bottom The sketch and cross section illustrate the new work: the reconstruction of the dome, the new wing of the Parliament building, the glass wall and the enormous cone of mirrors for natural daylighting inside the Reichstag.

94 left Norman Foster's renovation work did not touch the democratic inscription "Dem Deutschen Volke," which was left as a memory of the past and a caveat for the future.

94-95 Foster's restoration revived the splendor of the seat of German democracy, associating the old walls of the Parliament with the innovative appearance of the dome.

DESIGN	CONSTRUCTION	DIMENSIONS	USE
N. FOSTER	1995-1999	TOTAL AREA 658,385 SQUARE FEET	PARLIAMENT BUILDING

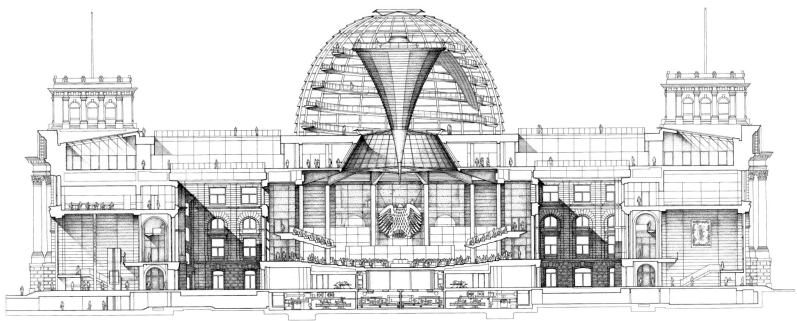

The Reichstag

96 and 96-97 The mirrors covering the "light sculptor" capture sunlight and reflect it into the assembly chamber. In accordance with the institutions, Foster designed this part of the building to make it accessible to the public, as it symbolizes the transparency of the institutions and represents the participation of citizens in public life. A helical ramp, which starts at the observation platform overlooking the Parliament chamber, is anchored to the structure of the dome and coils upwards to bring visitors to the top of the "lantern".

approach to the building would have been to gut it and insert a modern building in it. The more the building was probed, however, the stronger the marks of history emerged, making it unthinkable to obliterate them.

The transformation of the building was based on four guiding principles: first; the importance of the Bundestag as a democratic forum; second, maximum public accessibility to the workings of government; third, sensitivity to the importance of history; and fourth, rigorous environmental sustainability. The reconstruction project thus focused on restoring the windows and entrance, and on recovering the original structure of the building.

The main entrance was reopened on the west side, for use by both the public and politicians, and the monumental staircase that leads up to the building offers striking views of the offices of the Parliamentary President and the Chancellor.

This has been achieved through the extensive use of glass. In fact, the entire new construction inside the historic building is made of glass, in order to make all its internal activities visible.

The first floor houses the Parliament chamber, with 750 seats – one for each member – divided by party affiliation. The second floor holds the rooms of the President and the Council of Ministers, and the third floor houses the party meeting rooms.

Above this is a terrace, and from here visitors can access a restaurant and the glass dome.

The dome towers above the monumental building of the Reichstag, adding to its majesty and the importance of its role.

Two helical ramps allow visitors to climb the dome to the observation platform above the chamber, placing them physically and symbolically above political power.

97 bottom The view of the city from the top of the dome is breathtaking. Visitors feel as if they have been projected skywards, and enjoy a 360-degree view of the entire cityscape. This level is about 45 meters from the ground, and it is easy to image the sense of awe inspired by the glass dome and the panorama.

98 Subdued neutral shades have been used for the Parliament chamber, and the only splash of color is the blue of the upholstered seats, which changes with the intensity of the light shining on the fabric.

99 top and bottom right The Parliament chamber is elevated by about 5 feet in order to accommodate the tiered seating arrangement. Twelve concrete columns support the outer ring of the dome, and twelve brackets extend from the columns to sustain the inner ring and the cone of mirrors.

99 bottom left The plan view shows the piano nobile, the main floor of the Parliament.

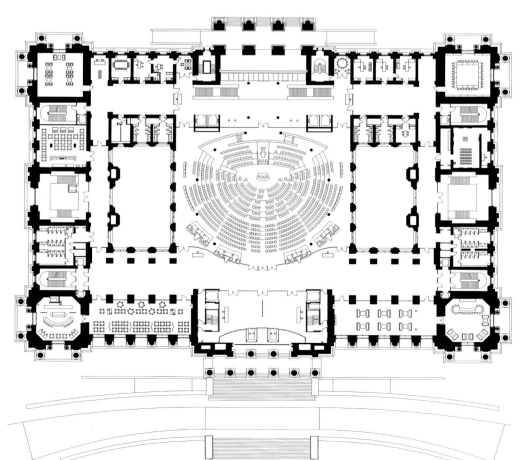

The Reichstag

100-101 and 101 The design of the dome stems mainly from its function as a bearer of light, and secondly from its role as an active element in the building's new energy system. The dome is the most important part of this system. First of all, its daylighting function saves considerable energy. Secondly, it also ventilates the Parliament chamber through a system installed inside the glass cone. Fresh air is brought into the building through the west portico, because the winds in Berlin blow mainly from this direction. It is then channeled into ducts that go to the chamber, where it is diffused through holes in the flooring. The heated air rises to the ceiling, where it is captured by the cone through air vents. At this point, the pressure differential that is generated drives the air out through the upper part of the cone on top of the dome.

The Reichstag

The dome is 75 feet high and 230 feet across. Its overall weight exceeds 1300 tons – including the 770-ton steel framework – and it is entirely double-glazed.

For the Reichstag, Foster again used an exoskeleton in order to create a structure without any supporting elements that might break up the form of the building. In the case of the dome, the frame not only supports the dome itself, but also the helical ramps, the observation platform, and the central cone.

The dome is not merely the distinguishing element of the project from an architectural standpoint, symbolizing the lightness, transparency, and permeability of government, but also a fundamental technological feature in terms of the use of energy and light.

The heart of the dome houses the "light sculptor," a truncated cone that extends from the top of the dome to perforate the ceiling of the Parliament chamber. The scale of the structure is impressive: the larger base, set inside the dome, measures over 52 feet across, while the diameter of the smaller base exceeds 8 feet. Its total weight is 330 tons. The cone is covered with 360 highly reflective glass mirrors and equipped with a computer-driven mobile shield (powered by photovoltaic cells) that blocks out heat and filters the sunlight.

The function of the "light sculptor" is to absorb sunlight by means of angular mirrors, and diffuse it in the assembly chamber, while the mobile shield follows the rotation of the sun to prevent the penetration of heat and filter direct light. The shield is not used during the winter and when the sun is low on the horizon, thus allowing the direct penetration of sunlight.

At night the opposite process occurs: when the Bundestag is in session, the lights of the assembly hall are reflected on the "light sculptor," illuminating the dome.

However, the truncated cone does not simply illuminate the building. It is also part of the ventilation system of the Parliament chamber, as its structure funnels warm air from the room, while axial fans and heat exchangers recycle energy from the waste air. Fresh air, drawn in from outside through the portico on the west side of the building, enters the chamber through the floor, thus reducing both drafts and noise.

The building boasts an extraordinarily radical energy strategy. The energy required to operate the ventilation system and drive the mobile shield of the dome is provided by 100 solar-power modules with photovoltaic cells located on the roof, generating approximately 40 kW of energy.

The electricity needed to run the entire building is produced by a cogenerator that burns vegetable oil made from date palms and sunflower seeds, which is as efficient as traditional fuel but reduces carbon dioxide emissions by 94%. Surplus heat is stored as hot water in an aquifer almost 1000 feet below ground and can be pumped up to heat the building.

The Reichstag can thus be considered an example of sustainable architecture, both in terms of its use of natural light and ventilation, and in its utilization of renewable energy sources. With this building, Foster has once again demonstrated the link between architecture and the environment, which have become inseparable in modern architecture. (Alessandra Di Marco)

The DG Bank

BERLIN, GERMANY

In recent years Berlin has come to symbolize a city entirely dedicated to the future, in which the reconstruction undertaken following reunification has deleted the city's past as an emblem of separation between East and West to replace it with an architectural workshop and a buzzing cultural center.

However, Berlin is not just a city of gleaming modern

buildings, for it still retains its history, despite sweeping demolition. Its historic district is centered on the Brandenburger Tor, the famous Brandenburg Gate overlooking the Pariser Platz (Paris Place) in what was formerly East Berlin, which once marked the divide between the two parts of the city.

The DG Bank headquarters are situated in the heart of the new embassy district of Berlin, in a mixed-use building that also houses 39 apartments overlooking the recently remodeled square and gardens.

The building occupies the maximum space permitted by the rectangular plot and is inserted lengthwise among the surrounding buildings, adapting itself to the form of the Pariser Platz and presenting a very distinctive dynamic façade on the Behrenstrasse.

The large building connects three perfectly harmonized and complementary parts: the two monumental stone façades, with completely different characters, and the large central atrium of the bank, which juxtaposes light, translucent and luminous materials in a dynamic dance, creating a vibrant zoomorphic composition that is the hallmark of Frank Gehry.

The DG Bank is accessed from the Pariser Platz. The façade is marked by the alternation of large windows set in massive and simply dressed squared slabs of yellow Vicenza stone The linear arrangement echoes the rhythms and proportions of the surrounding buildings. The recessed windows adapt the structure to the severe appearance of the square, and the articulation of the façade in deep bays gives it a sculptural quality. The impressive dimensions of the stone blocks called for specially designed cutting and anchorage processes in order to meet the structural challenge of bearing the weight of the huge monoliths and solve the problem of the fragility of the stone.

On the opposite side of the plot, the façade of the ten-story residential complex with 39 apartments has an undulating motion that evokes some of Gaudí's buildings.

The great dynamism of the south façade is marked by the dynamic succession of recessed balconies and is further enhanced by steel bow windows set into the warm surface of the stone.

The cladding is formed by stone slabs of various sizes. The

102 top The façade on Pariser Platz, rhythmically punctuated by the sequence of enormous blocks of yellow Vicenza stone, creates an image of solid stability, emphasized by the windows whose frames seem to disappear in the curtain wall.

102 center The enormous glass dome, which has an area of nearly 20,000 square feet, covers the atrium at the eave line. The structure is composed of a metal grid with a triangular web that billows over the interior space.

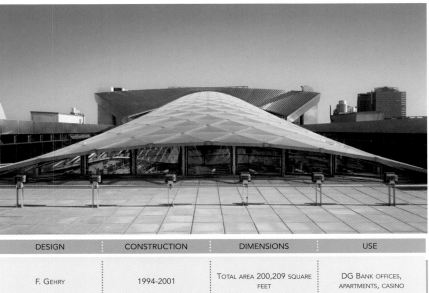

102 bottom Staggered floors and stainless-steel bow windows can be seen on the Behrenstrasse façade, made of stone slabs of different sizes. To ensure perfect insulation, the cladding was laid after the bow windows were installed.

102-103 and 103 bottom Topped by the stainless-steel web, the rooftop room enjoys a fabulous view of Brandenburg Gate, the Reichstag and the Tiergarten.

DESIGN	CONSTRUCTION	DIMENSIONS	USE
F. GEHRY	1994-2001	TOTAL AREA 200,209 SQUARE FEET	DG BANK OFFICES, APARTMENTS, CASINO

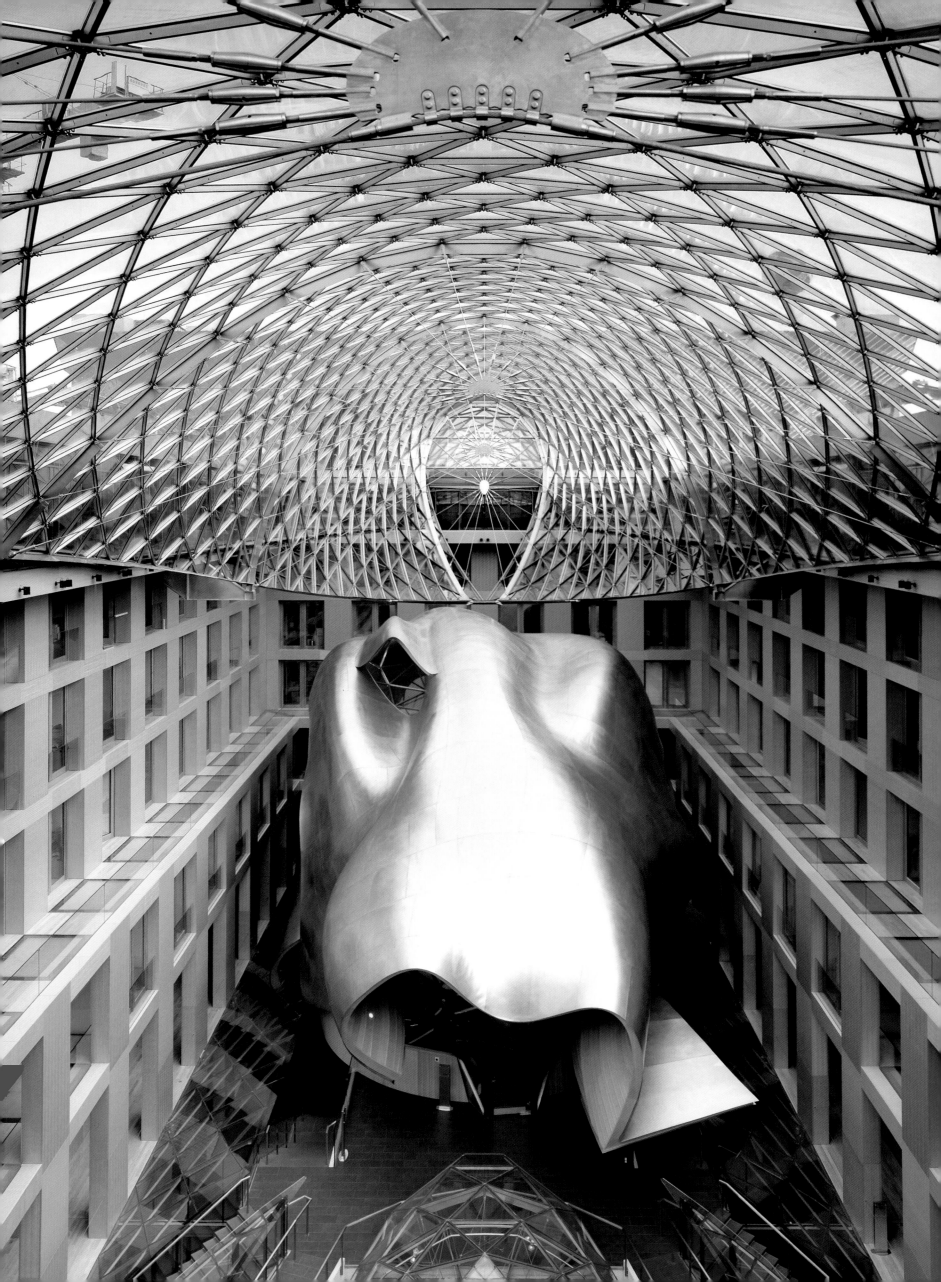

The DG Bank

104 The glass-and-steel roof over the enormous atrium resembles a spider web and envelops the space, highlighting the sculptural volume of the "horse's head."

105 top The initial curvature of the glass ceiling is progressively modified so that it tapers to end on an elliptical plane that slopes inward.

105 bottom A wooden arcade leads to the office lobbies and extends on both sides of the atrium, overlooking it to take advantage of the natural light that streams in through the glass ceiling. The glass floor of the balcony allows light to reach every office floor.

base is faced with slabs that measure up to 47 by 59 inches, while smaller ones, with a maximum size of 30 by 51 inches, were used for the upper part of the façade. Pin systems with special aluminum alloy brackets were required to anchor the blocks of stone. The cladding was applied after the windows had been set in place in order to ensure perfect insulation.

Both façades are clad with limestone in a color close to that of the Brandenburg Gate, playing a fundamental role in establishing a rapport between the building and its surroundings. At the same time, they trigger a dichotomy between interior and exterior, and between heavy materials and gleaming lightweight ones, by blending opposite construction cultures: crafted stone versus high-tech steel and glass.

However, the discretion of the façades is a screen to conceal the inversion of solids and voids of a fluid and transparent interior space.

Passing through the foyer and a lobby, one reaches the large inner courtyard covered by a curved skylight. This area, measuring 200 by 66 feet, acts as a light well for the surrounding six stories of bank offices, which overlook this space dilated by the gossamer mesh ceiling that sets the scene for a theatrical representation of volumes and transparencies, in a succession of forms that daze, disorient, and astonish the observer.

The roof is formed by a shell with a stainless-steel skeleton, which bends, billows and changes appearance, assuming an elliptical form in a plane set diagonally towards the interior.

The most complex aspect in the creation of this structure did not involve the design or construction stages, but the

106 top The membrane of the clear floor puffs up to illuminate the underground areas of the casino and the cafeteria.

106 bottom The wooden interior of the horse's head contrasts the metal shell of the exterior.

107 From the ceiling of the cafeteria, located below the floor of the atrium, the two clear membranes overlap to form a double "heavenly vault" that vertically expands this space. The curvature of the roof accentuates the sense of dynamic tension.

The DG Bank

onsite installation of the various preassembled parts.

This immense transparent roof is a triangular glass-and-steel web covering an area of almost 20,000 square feet. The functional division of space has been solved by interposing a 12,000-square-foot clear glass floor on the entrance level of the bank. It dialogues with the atrium skylight to create an interior space set between two ethereal partitions that are curved to contain a colossal sculpture.

The "horse's head," as it is commonly known, is a huge sculptural element in gleaming steel sheeting that floats in the imposing space of the atrium and houses a 100-seat conference room beneath its base. It was created by combining sophisticated digital design with metalworking. The structure unites a sequence of iron elements that form the skeleton and a covering of three-dimensional, modeled steel sheets pieced together like the tiles of a mosaic. The interior is clad with perforated wooden strips combined with glass partitions that close the holes.

The first- and second-floor offices overlook the atrium, with a view of the imposing space through balconies with transparent floors. The offices, meeting rooms and private dining rooms on the upper floors instead enjoy extraordinary views of Brandenburg Gate and the Reichstag through the high ceilings and sloping north-facing walls.

The basement, which is visible through the glass floor, houses a casino that can accommodate 225 people, contrasting with the seriousness of the building's banking function and offering a place for transgression, in a reversal of trend that mirrors the designer's wish to harmonize material, stylistic and functional contrasts.

The atrium of the bank is divided from the apartments by a third glass partition that contrasts with the concave concrete wall and takes the form of an enormous convex lens that is ten stories high, which concentrates the zenithal light from the large almond-shaped skylight above the atrium of the apartments. The vertical atrium acts as a lobby for the apartments and provides the residential block with natural lighting and ventilation.

The rooftop restaurant affords simultaneous views of the sculptural complexity of the atrium, the Pariser Platz and Brandenburg Gate, and further away, the Reichstag, taking in at a glance the contamination of periods and compositional languages that coexist in this context. (Guya Elisabetta Rosso)

T. VAN DEN VALENTYN

H. HOLLEIN

Städtisches Museum Abteiberg

MÖNCHENGLADBACH, GERMANY

108 top The building designed to house the museum administration has a "dual personality." The back, which establishes a rapport with the existing buildings, is composed of a continuous curtain wall made of marble slabs, whereas the front, which faces the new square, is a clear glass wall.

108 bottom The museum extends deep into the heart of the hillside. This space is illuminated by 7 sandstone "boxes" set over the permanent collection and by the block of 16 skylights over the space devoted to temporary exhibits.

When the planned-for new museum commenced in 1972, Mönchengladbach was a city with approximately 200,000 inhabitants. A few years later, it merged with the nearby town of Rheydt to become an important urban hub. Mönchengladbach is situated to the west of a leading industrial and cultural area comprising cities such as Cologne, Essen, Düsseldorf, and Dortmund.

The city's museum tradition goes back to 1904, when the wealthy bourgeoisie of the textile industry opened a local history museum. In 1922 a private collector donated a collection of expressionist works to the museum, effectively transforming it into an art gallery. Following the arrival of the new director, Johannes Cladders, in 1967, and a new openness toward contemporary art, the decision was made to build a new museum appropriate for these works. Cladders personally contacted Hans Hollein to design the new premises. The director was convinced that the museum space should have a well-defined character, and not merely constitute a neutral container for the works of art, as their setting also influences their message and the emotions that they can convey. Hollein accepted the commission for what was his first large building.

The close relationship between the works of art and the museum structure implies that the strength of the building is its interior space, whose success is dependent on the diversity of lighting, heights, forms and materials. However, the same diversity applied to the exterior generates a complex and articulate structure that may even seem contradictory at first glance.Hollein used many different materials – brick, stone, concrete, marble, aluminum, bronze, steel, brass and lead – combined in a miscellaneous collection of buildings. The museum is situated on top of a hill, in the historic district of the city, and is juxtaposed with the most diverse buildings: a church, an office block, a chapel, an industrial warehouse, and a park.

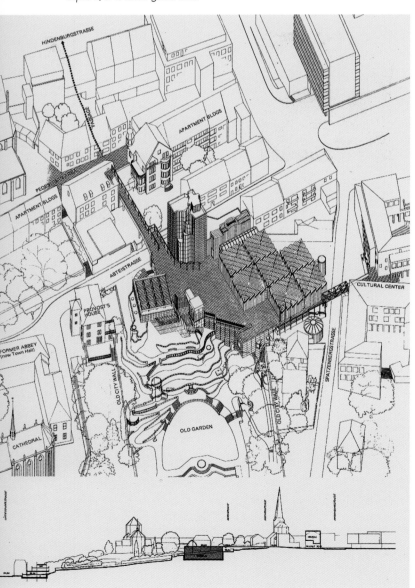

108-109 The museum is situated on the south slope of a small hill, on top of which is the historic district of Mönchengladbach.

This city is not far from Düsseldorf and Cologne. The gardens are incorporated in the museum structure.

DESIGN	CONSTRUCTION	DIMENSIONS	USE
H. HOLLEIN T. VAN DER VALENTYN	1972-1982	TOTAL AREA 78,577 SQUARE FT	CONTEMPORARY ART MUSEUM

Städtisches Museum Abteiberg

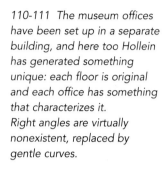

110-111 The museum offices have been set up in a separate building, and here too Hollein has generated something unique: each floor is original and each office has something that characterizes it.
Right angles are virtually nonexistent, replaced by gentle curves.

110 bottom On the hillside, the retaining walls – undulating, flowing and sinuous – contrast sharply with the rigidity of the museum structures that emerge from the ground.

111 top The rigidity of the sandstone skylights offsets the flexibility of the path of light that

separates the public space of the square from the tower with the administrative offices.

111 bottom On the stone laid at the entrance to the museum, Hans Hollein engraved his name, followed by the year the work commenced and the year the museum was inaugurated.

The museum entrance is situated in the center of the complex and is constituted by a marble and glass pavilion. In the most traditional conception of art, the path leading to knowledge is generally uphill, but in this case Hollein has built a downhill entrance. The access leads to an underground space pervaded by both natural and artificial light, whose nature and intensity varies according to the complexity of the individual spaces.

There is no set visiting itinerary and visitors are free to move in any direction within the museum. The layout of the spaces generates junctions and thus uncertainty, with the need to make personal choices instead of following a reassuring route

established by others. All the circulation areas, such as the staircases, are different, sparking wonder and curiosity. Each area has been designed according to the type of work that it would house, and from colors and shape to lighting, nothing has been left to chance.

While the dominant – and indeed only – colors in the galleries are those of the works of art, the rest of the complex (offices, lecture halls, reading room, video room, etc.) uses rich, bold colors such as reds and greens, checkered patterns on floors and ceilings, decorated doors and closets, and furniture of all shapes and colors. (Alessandra di Marco)

112-113 and 113 top The museum space is divided into three underground floors. The first one exploits the daylight pouring in through the skylights, whereas artificial lighting systems were designed for the other two.

113 center and bottom The characteristics and proportions of each exhibition room are the result of extensive research into the artwork that would be displayed in it. In some cases,

visitors are in close contact with the work, in a cozy and contemplative space, whereas in others the space is so large that it can hold numerous works and thus offer an overall view of the collection.

All the exhibition spaces are linked by color: white plaster for the walls and white marble for the floors. This creates a neutral backdrop where the artwork can be displayed at its best.

Städtisches Museum Abteiberg

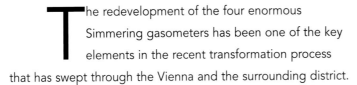
Gasometer City

VIENNA, AUSTRIA

The redevelopment of the four enormous Simmering gasometers has been one of the key elements in the recent transformation process that has swept through the Vienna and the surrounding district.

Built in the late 1900s, the four buildings were part of the city's gas production and distribution plant, which also housed offices and utilities, as well as a water tower for regulating tank pressure. The gasometers, which have an outside diameter of 213 feet and a total height of nearly 230 feet, were built along the Danube Canal. On the four cylindrical tanks – oversized examples of industrial archaeology – enormous quadrants indicating the amount of gas contained in them were juxtaposed with molding and various orders of two-light and small windows.

114 top From a height of 230 feet, the industrial architecture of the past contemplates the technological changes that have swept through Vienna.

114 center The glass dome of the roof filters natural light to illuminate the interior of the courtyard, which is lined with offices and residences.

114 bottom In Coop Himmelb(l)au's preliminary sketches, the deconstructivist slant that the two Viennese architects give their buildings is evident. The key to interpreting the meaning of their works comes from the symbolic mobility they represent.

115 Coop Himmelb(l)au intervened with "added volume": a building that creates a sharp contrast with the existing structure, and contains residences and offices in a wide array of sizes.

DESIGN	CONSTRUCTION	DIMENSIONS	USE
Coop Himmelb(l)au W.D. Prix H.Swiczinsky	1995-2001	Total area 376,737 square feet	Residential, office and community service complex

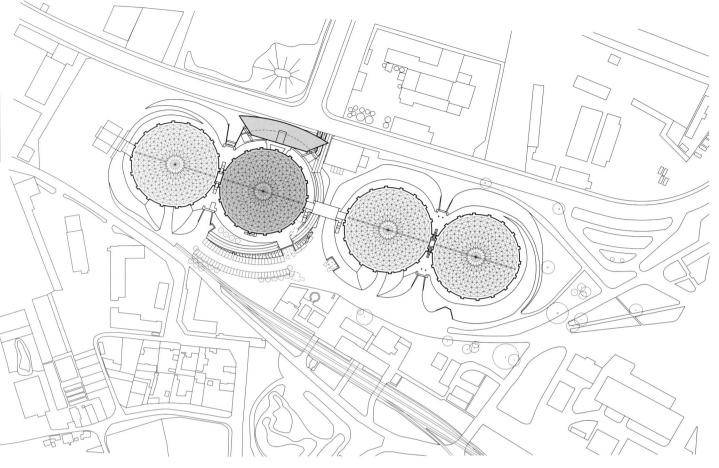

The property was abandoned in 1984, when methane replaced gas, but in 1995 the municipality decided to restore and redevelop the old plant, conserving its historical façade and metal roofing structure. The architectural firms of Jean Nouvel, Coop Himmelb(l)au, Manfred Wehdorn and Wilhelm Holzbauer were commissioned to design the four new buildings.

Gasometer B by Coop Himmelb(l)au is part of a new context that is now known as G-Town, or Gasometer City. The original structure of nearly 92,000 cubic feet of bricks and over 600 tons of steel has been replaced by 602 apartments (230 for students and the remainder as low-income housing), a shopping center (70 shops), a conference hall / auditorium (4200 seats), the National Archives of Vienna, and various services such as a daycare center, a multiplex cinema and a subway station.

The plans call for three separate volumes: the round one enclosing an internal patio, a multipurpose service center on

Gasometer City

116 G-Town is the immense complex composed of four old gasometers, which were used to store city gas until 1984 and have now been converted into a multipurpose apartment and commercial complex. They are 236 feet tall and about 203 feet across, and are connected to each other on the ground level by the shopping mall.

116-117 The "sky lobby" on the roof of the sixth floor is reserved for the residents' social activities.

Gasometer City

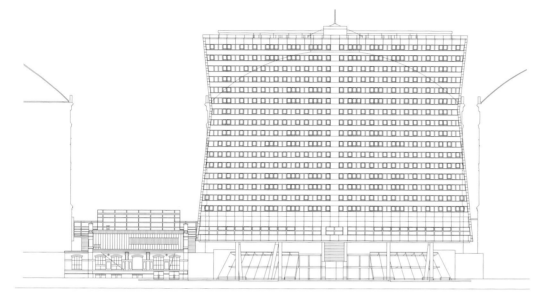

119 center and bottom The 18 floors of the building are crossed by elevators and stairs that separate the functions of the internal areas, composed of apartments and offices. The concrete piers that elevate it from the ground also serve as an entrance to the 4000-seat multipurpose room in the main building.

118 The powerful technological impact of the "wing," accentuated by the materials used to build it, is also evident in the interior of this structure, which features all the latest equipment. The homes, offices and shops are connected via an Intranet, which can also be connected directly to the Internet.

119 top As shown by the model, though the gap between the two buildings is very narrow, it receives natural light through an interplay of reflections and transparency.

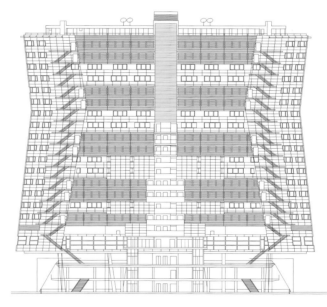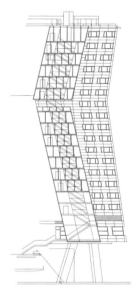

the ground floor, and the surprising "shield," a 19-story building with apartments and office space.

As separate languages of a single body, they eloquently evoke the evolution from the Industrial Age to the Information Age. They also mirror an on-the-go society and condition: the individual buildings owe their importance to their connections with a broader reality that takes the urban fabric, aesthetic perception and social function into consideration.

In the words of Wolf D. Prix and Helmut Swiczinsky, cofounders of the Austrian architectural firm Coop Himmelb(l)au, this goal has been achieved by creating architecture "that bleeds, exhausts, turns, and even breaks." Like its surroundings, the building is also distinguished by mobility. It is an organism on an urban scale, one that is no longer tied solely to its original function but in which the very

functions of buildings, the areas allocated to public and private, intersect to create a new image of space and new potential for use.

The disciplinary concept and underpinnings of the Modern Movement, whereby form follows function, thus fall to the wayside. Both can be independent or interdependent in ways that differ from traditional ones.

The principle that interior space must find expression outside and vice-versa is rejected to embrace their potential indifference or complementarity. Likewise, the assumption that the edifice is the expression of a structure with parts that are interrelated, albeit through dissonance, is countered by another more liberating one: that the parts can simply be drawn together and juxtaposed, as if to build the sky, as the very name of this architectural duo suggests. (Marco Tagliatori)

Gasometer City

120 top The large internal patio was created in place of the metal tank that once stored city gas, obtained by heating coal at extremely high temperatures. The gasometers were abandoned in 1984.

120 bottom and 120-121 The symbol of a new lifestyle, the gasometer complex offers a number of facilities: a cinema, cafés and restaurants, shops with over 235,000 square feet of floor space, and the shopping center that crosses and connects all four buildings.

121 bottom left The drawing illustrates the variety of activities offered by Gasometer B: the enormous multipurpose hall, the shopping center and a youth hostel on the lower floors.

121 bottom right The cutaway illustration shows the large multipurpose hall situated at the base of the building, whose foyer is connected directly to the subway station. The hall can seat 4000 people.

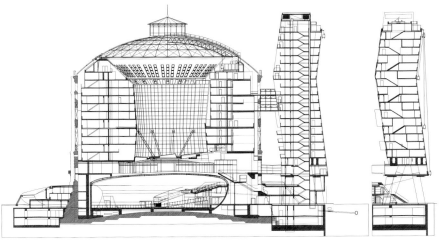

The Nationale-Nederlanden Building
PRAGUE, CZECH REPUBLIC

In Prague's historic district, where construction is strictly regulated to ensure conservation, the Nationale-Nederlanden Building , an office complex overlooking the Vltava River, is an extraordinary exception to the rule. The building, which Frank O. Gehry's firm initially dubbed "the wave," belies its initial impression, standing with subtle elegance amidst the nineteenth-century buildings along the river.

Backed by President Vaclav Havel and relied on the collaboration of the locally based Studio Vladimir Milunic, the project is complex in scope, combining business functions with the offices on the upper floors.

The Nationale-Nederlanden building was constructed on a square lot that had been vacant for years, as the building that once stood there was destroyed by a bomb in 1945. The lot thus acquires new spatial meaning, projecting the intersection of the two streets towards the river, and representing Prague's desire to invent a new language as a way of leaving the past behind by evolving – but without denying historical memory.

The complex, has shops and cafés on the ground floor, and offices from the second to the seventh floors. There is a rooftop restaurant with a stunning view of the city and Prague Castle.

The theme of the corner lot is a topic of experimentation in and of itself, and it has been resolved here by making it a focal and transition point in several ways. The building is composed of two extremely different structures. The riverside façade is aligned with those of the buildings adjacent to it, taking up their rhythm yet also varying it with undulating stringcourses.

The building is the same height as the ones next to it. While the other buildings are five stories high, however, the modern needs of the new structure called for seven floors. Gehry staggered the windows along the façade to tone down these differences and conceal the insertion of the two additional floors, which are recessed with respect to the front of the building.

DESIGN	CONSTRUCTION	DIMENSIONS	USE
F. Gehry	1992 - 1996	Typical floor area: 58,125 square feet	Offices, café-bar and restaurant

122 top The "Dancing House" is at the corner of two heavily trafficked streets. The entrance colonnade, which extends beyond the line of the building, makes the interaction between pedestrians and vehicles even more difficult by occupying a considerable portion of the sidewalk, where cars tend to speed past. Despite this traffic problem, the pedestrian tunnel proposed by Vladimir Milunic was rejected by the city authorities that approved the project.

122 bottom and 123 Before starting construction and during the creative process, Frank O. Gehry visited Prague several times, accompanied by Vladimir Milunic who acted as his guide, in order to grasp and assimilate the essence of the city. The architect came away with the impression that Prague's buildings were designed with "implied towers" and that because of the habit of crowning them with small calottes, "each building wears a hat."

The Nationale-Nederlanden Building

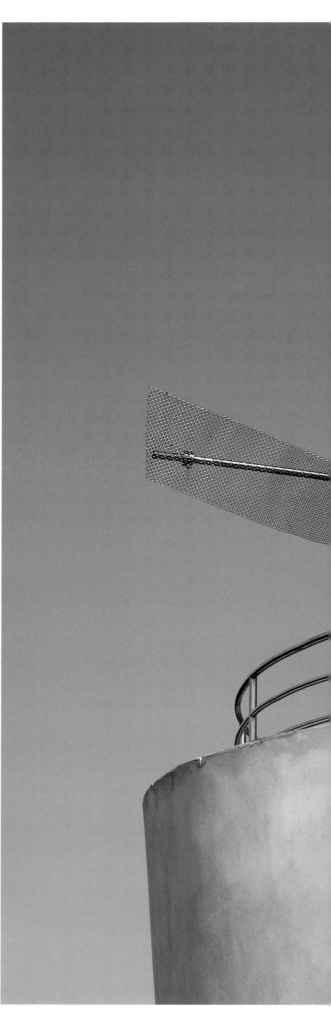

124 top Inspired by the sensations the city conveyed to him, Gehry designed two towers that are projected towards the outside and cling to the square.

124 center and bottom The restaurant overlooks the city and the Vltava River as well as the metal sphere set on top of the masonry tower.

124-125 With its twisted coil of metal bands conveying extraordinary sculptural dynamism, the sphere seems to be in perpetual motion.

126 and 127 top From the interior of the glass tower, which has meeting rooms on each floor and is awash in light, the city shows off all its beauty, imbued with history and culture.

127 bottom At the base of the sphere, the round skylight, which evokes the oculus of the Pantheon in Rome, offers a view of the sky from the interior of the metal structure.

The Nationale-Nederlanden Building

The wave created by the windows of the main façade culminates in the corner structure, a masonry tower that, like many of Prague's traditional buildings, is crowned by a cusped element – in this case a spherical structure composed of metal bands.

Rising alongside the solid masonry portion is a transparent tower that is tapered in the middle. The result is a structure that virtually quivers with dynamic tension, earning the building the monikers of the "Dancing House" and "Fred and Ginger." Indeed, it calls to mind the image of two twirling dancers, drawing the entire building into this movement.

In reality, the glass-clad tower was not designed to evoke a particular image and its pinch-waisted form reflects Gehry's desire to ensure that the adjacent buildings would have a view

of the Vltava. The sculptural columns along the entrance portico, arranged in seemingly random order, effectively extend the building to the very edge of the street, influencing pedestrian traffic and incorporating public space, which thus becomes part of the foot of the building. Each story of the glass tower has meeting rooms, creating a functional reference between the floors.

Bringing such innovative architecture to a setting like Prague sparked enormous debate. Great attention to cultural dialogue was required to establish a sense of harmony between the new features of Gehry's architecture and its historic surroundings. The "Dancing House" is thus an powerful example of how new architectural languages can be incorporated in traditional settings. (Guya Elisabetta Rosso)

DESIGN	CONSTRUCTION	DIMENSIONS	USE
S. Calatrava	1993-1998	Track area: 43,917 square feet	Railroad interchange station

Oriente Station

LISBON, PORTUGAL

The district of Olivais was the focus of the World Exposition held in Lisbon in 1998 to commemorate the 500th anniversary of the discovery of the sea route to India by Vasco da Gama, an event that marked the beginning of great urban expansion and Portugal's emergence as its own entity.

Following the end of the colonial empire in 1974 and Portugal's entry to the European Union in 1986, Lisbon recovered its ancient political and economic links with the continent and returned to being the symbolic meeting point between East and West, land and sea.

Just as the city plays a vital role in the exchange of cultures, memories and challenges, the site chosen for the Expo represents the hinge between the city and the Tagus, a desolate industrial area wedged between the railroad and the riverbanks, which was chosen to represent the transition between past and future.

This is the setting for the Oriente Station, which was built to expand the urban transport infrastructures for the Exposition. The complex structure was designed with the dual function of constituting the entrance to the Expo for visitors arriving from all over Europe and acting as a driving force for redevelopment of the adjoining area.

Calatrava's winning design was superimposed on the existing railroad line, which runs along the western side of the site on a thirty-foot embankment and separates the residential and industrial areas, thus forming a complex that acts as a modern intermodal terminal and resolving the internal division of the city by reconnecting the urban fabric through the station entrances on the east and west sides of the railroad.

It is arranged on three levels, which comprise all the functions associated with transportation: underground parking, a taxi terminal, a bus station, and a stopping and transit area for subway, regional, and international trains.

Outside, the raised course of the tracks is clearly visible, in the form of a 290-foot-long railroad bridge whose supporting structure acts as an element of continuity for the three areas of the station. The underground level forms the central hall of

the concourse, which is the transit area for all the routes. This triple-height space is marked off by balconies and walkways that are connected by escalators and form inner floors housing services for travelers and shops. This animal-like structure, resembling a powerful reinforced-concrete skeleton, extends vertically at street level with the long rippling steel-and-glass roofs of the platforms of the bus terminal, supported by cement trusses and connected to each other by a raised walkway. The complex is topped by the roof of the railroad platforms, resembling an oasis of slender palms of white steel and glass sheltering travelers from the broiling Mediterranean sun.

The building's sculptural monumentality, expressionism

128 top, 128-129 and 129 bottom right Slender forms in white steel and laminated glass: the silhouette of the Oriente

Station stands out majestically. This intermodal interchange hub is the new gateway to the Lisbon of the future.

129 bottom left The station reconnects the urban fabric of the 1998 Exposition site, and the entrances beneath the

elevated platforms also link the old city with the new complex, both practically and symbolically.

130-131 Laid out on three interchange levels, the railroad station looks like an oasis protected by slender palms of white steel, rising to a height of 30 feet. Though the station is seemingly fragmented due to the use of highly differentiated materials for the various functional elements, it nevertheless evokes an extraordinary sense of lightness and simplicity.

131 top and bottom Elevators emerge from the ground to lead to the subway station; the entrances and bus terminals are on the street level.

131 center The station – a modern Gothic cathedral and the temple of travelers – was designed not only to serve a technical purpose but also as a place where people meet and socialize.

Oriente Station

and forms magnify Calatrava's artistic approach to this project. Here, structural elements create continuous and controlled movement, tracing fine lines of static equilibrium through space, with organic elements that form the composition as a whole and emphasize its transparency. However, it is not an isolated building: connected to the surrounding urban fabric through the fusion of tradition, technology and remembrance of place, it creates a large public area in which people live and meet. (Marco Tagliatori)

132 top To model the forms of the sculptural shell enclosing the building, the architect decided to clad this urban-scale sculpture with titanium plating, used with galvanized steel and lined with tar paper.

132 bottom For the stone parts, nearly 33,000 square yards of amber beige stone were quarried at Huéscar in the region of Granada. The slabs, which are 2 inches thick, were polished after they were laid.

The Guggenheim Museum

BILBAO, SPAIN

Originally a fishing port, Bilbao modified its urban vocation with the industrial development of the iron trade, and following the postindustrial economic crisis of 1985, the city has risen once more. The path chosen to redevelop the city involved promoting social change and undertaking urban transformation, starting with socioeconomic aspects.

As part of this innovation, the close collaboration between the Basque authorities and the Solomon R. Guggenheim Foundation ultimately made the museum the linchpin of urban renewal that affected the entire city. In fact, as part of its redevelopment plan, Bilbao has commissioned works by some of the leading names in contemporary architecture.

Situated in a former business and industrial district, the Guggenheim Museum Bilbao represented the first step towards revitalizing the city. The area is well connected with the central

thus making the Guggenheim an important part of city life.

A ramp along the river leads to the sculptural tower. As disjointed as a cardboard castle, the tower was designed as an element of integration, also serving as a public pedestrian route linking the site to the rest of the city.

The plaza leads to the enormous central atrium, which organizes and distributes the flow of visitors. The three concentric floors of exhibition galleries extend from here. The atrium, which covers an area of nearly 7000 square feet, is the heart of the museum. It was inspired by the expressionist constructions of Fritz Lang's film *Metropolis*, but the principles of Brancusi's sculptures can also be discerned here. The galleries, arranged in ascending spirals, evoke the Guggenheim Museum in New York. The ceiling ends in a sculptured metal "flower" skylight that lets in natural light to create a warm and welcoming space. The enormous glass walls of the atrium draw

and historic districts, and is effectively a hub with respect to the city's main cultural and administrative buildings, such as City Hall, the University of the Basque Country and the Fine Arts Museum. At the same time, however, it has also become a rendezvous and the starting point of a cultural itinerary.

The large plaza in front of the entrance encourages pedestrian traffic between the Guggenheim and the Fine Arts Museum, and between the historic district and the Nervión riverfront. A number of shops and businesses line the plaza, and they can also be accessed from the interior of the museum,

133 The thickness of the titanium plates – just 16/1000 of an inch – could have created problems, such as being lifted by wind. To minimize the problem, the 66 tons of metal were shaped using a special lamination process in order to form 33,000 metal scales. Several different countries were involved in this complex procedure: the metal was mined in Austria, cast in France and laminated in the United States (Pittsburgh).

DESIGN	CONSTRUCTION	DIMENSIONS	USE
F. Gehry	1993-1997	Total area 265,008 square feet	Museum, administrative offices, square, aquatic garden

The Guggenheim Museum

134-135 Gehry has perfected a fascinating technique to mold the sculptural forms typical of his works. His sketches and studies are loaded into a computer to analyze them mathematically and find the right structural answers.

134 bottom The bridges suspended across the cavernous central atrium help create a multifaceted environment, and they also permit access to the interior of the façade to make it easier to clean the windows.

135 left The enormous central atrium is the hub from which the museum areas extend. This space is a light well, illuminated by a huge window supported by a metal structure.

135 right In addition to major theme exhibits, solo shows and temporary exhibits, the museum displays a selection of works on loan from other institutions that are part of the Guggenheim Foundation. It also has an educational area that promotes learning through art.

the cityscape into the museum, effectively making it part of an ever-changing exhibition.

From the atrium, visitors can access the terrace, which is covered by a canopy supported by a single stone pillar. The terrace overlooks an artificial pool set above the river level.

The complexity conveyed by the exterior is deceptive, as Frank O. Gehry actually designed a relatively simple space, arranging the museum on three floors, plus one to house utilities.

The multifaceted shell of the museum is countered by the interior's extremely neutral architecture. This choice was dictated by the desire to facilitate comprehension of the works on display. The seemingly random combination of rooms differing in shape and size gives the museum a multipurpose character that is unrivalled around the world.

permanent and temporary collections. The service and utility areas are on the lower level.

The construction materials are also distinguished based on function. The solidity of the stone used for the rectilinear forms offsets the fluidity of the sculptural curvilinear forms clad in titanium panels. The use of titanium, which has a high light-reflection coefficient, dramatically alters the appearance of the façades, depending on the time of day: silvery at dawn, dazzlingly lucent at noon, and gilded at sunset.

The lighting of the different spaces has been structured based on exhibition needs and the shapes of the rooms. Recessed wall lighting has been used for the permanent collection, whereas the lighting system in the less conventional spaces of the gallery for temporary exhibits and for the works of living artists is suspended

The Guggenheim Foundation asked the architect to create varied exhibition spaces to accommodate the different collections it wanted to exhibit at the new museum. Gehry responded to this need by creating three types of rooms. The ones for the permanent collection and those for the temporary exhibits are rectilinear, the former housed in two adjoining square spaces on the second and third floors, and the latter in a dramatic rectangular gallery along the east side, which connects the museum to the tower on the other side of the Puente de la Salve Bridge crossing the Nervión.

The interior is composed of a free space that can house large-scale installations. The collections by living artists are displayed in a series of curvilinear galleries with broad mezzanines at various points of the museum, so that they can be viewed in relation to the other works exhibited as part of the

from structures that resemble catwalks. Enormous skylights let in natural light, which can be adjusted via motorized shades.

World-renowned artists were commissioned to create sculptural installations for the Guggenheim Museum in Bilbao. Richard Serra's *Snake* is unquestionably one of the most famous of these site-specific works. Three enormous serpentine bands of steel – 102 feet long and 13 feet high – snake across the cavernous space of the El *Pez* or Fish Gallery. This work is so large that it even astonished Gehry, who had initially planned to break up this space. The imposing architecture of the Guggenheim Museum Bilbao makes it a container that is unique in size. For example, it has nearly 260,000 square feet of floor space – twice as much as the Beaubourg in Paris.

Unlike many other works that have a similar impact on their surroundings and have aroused debate and controversy,

particularly among residents, the stone-and-metal colossus that Gehry created in the Basque city has earned unanimous public and critical acclaim. The design of the building was powerfully influenced by its location. First of all, it evokes the materials historically used in the industrial constructions along the river. Likewise, the size and layout of the city were key elements in designing the museum, demonstrating profound respect for tradition. (Guya Elisabetta Rosso)

136-137 Special attention has been paid to the illumination of the artwork, and natural light never strikes them.

137 Gehry built a gallery that is about 425 feet long and 80 feet high to house large-scale works.

138-139 The philosophy of this institution is to avoid static displays. As a result, the dynamism of the museum's architecture is a metaphor for the ongoing transformation and evolution of its functions and of the installations housed inside it.

The City of Arts and Sciences

VALENCIA, SPAIN

The large complex dedicated to culture and science is part of an urban context gradually created in Valencia after 1957, when the course of the Turia River was diverted south of the city following disastrous flooding. This formed a strip of land five miles long and 650 feet wide that separates the old city from the seaside quarter of Nazaret. This large area was converted into a park between 1981 and 1988 by the architect Ricardo Bofill, whose project included creating green areas and lakes to evoke the former presence of the Turia, now reduced to a dry riverbed, as well as public areas, sports facilities, and a botanical garden.

This original complex was later extended, in 1987 and 2001 respectively, with José Maria de Paredes' Palau de la Musica and the Oceanogràfic, whose exposed roof structures were the last project of the late structural architect Felix Candela.

Subsequently, the city authorities decided to add a nationally prominent museum to this 85-acre area in order to emphasize the city's cultural importance. In 1991 Santiago Calatrava won the competition to construct a telecommunications tower on the western part of the site (replaced by the Palacio de las Artes in 1996). Soon after he was awarded the commission for the entire complex, which also includes a science museum and a planetarium.

The result is a city within the city, a cultural attraction whose purpose is to generate the same economic benefit experienced by Bilbao as a consequence of the new Guggenheim Museum designed by Frank O. Gehry. It was also devised to bring new focus to a disjointed and

140 top Art and technology are the two key concepts behind the success of this enormous educational structure, which is destined to become the symbol of Valencia, as it attracts 4 million visitors a year.

140 bottom The Oceanogràfic, designed by Felix Candela and built in 2001, is part of the complex of buildings composing the City. Like them, it is part of the redevelopment of the 5-mile strip.

140-141 and 141 bottom left The stately buildings, each of which has a specific purpose, are aligned from east to west. They seem to emerge from the surrounding pools like majestic extinct creatures.

DESIGN	CONSTRUCTION	DIMENSIONS	USE
S. CALATRAVA	1991-2005	TOTAL AREA 3,767,369 SQUARE FEET	PLANETARIUM, SCIENCE MUSEUM, AUDITORIUM

141 bottom right This ambitious project was commissioned and financed in 1991 by the Valencian government, or Generalitat. This Catalan term means "community," demonstrating the common desire to relaunch the city's cultural significance and absorb inevitable economic repercussions.

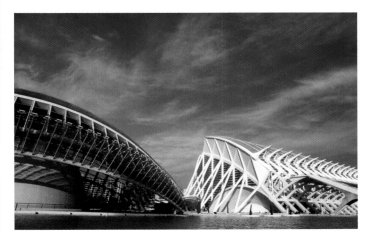

The City of Arts and Sciences

142 top The complex's elevated walkways offer unexpected and surprising views. The entrances to the stairways of the parking area also respect the overall design of the complex and have been inspired by forms present in nature.

142 bottom and 142-143 The Museum of Science, the second building to complete the sequence of the complex, overturns the traditional educational concept of exhibitions. Equipped with the

most advanced interactive systems, it merges education with entertainment – but without falling into the commercial trap of creating a theme park. The main rule of its director, Manuel Toharia, is: "Not touching the displayed objects is strictly forbidden." The exhibition area, which boasts more than 450,000 square feet of floor space, includes the collections bequeathed by Severo Ochoa, who won the Nobel Prize in Medicine.

underrated area that this large-scale project has transformed into a vibrant link between the city center and the sea.

The City of Arts and Sciences can undoubtedly be defined as the most complex, surprising, and colossal of Calatrava's works and has become one of those "landmarks" that – as politicians are well aware – can change the face of a city, introducing such powerful innovation that it ultimately becomes a symbol.

The predominant inspiration for the project is nature, as mother and teacher: the City's four buildings are all based on

biological forms, from the skeleton of a huge recumbent dinosaur that forms the science museum to the eye of the planetarium that observes the sky and, beyond, a petrified forest. The outstretched zoomorphic structures are reflected in the water that surrounds them, symbolizing the sea and doubling their already monumental dimensions like a Mediterranean Taj Mahal.

The inauguration of the Hemisfèric in 1998 attracted the complex's first public acclaim – and criticism. The planetarium emerges like a enormous shell from a pool (4265 feet long and 656 wide), which reflects and duplicates its image, transforming it into a giant human eye in which the dome of the IMAX cinema forms the pupil, protected by a monumental steel-and-glass eyelid that opens and closes to allow visitors to enter. Inside, an ultramodern computer-controlled astronomic projection system provides a complete representation of the sky and its celestial bodies on a surface measuring almost eighty feet across, tilted at a 30° angle.

The almost endless variations in lighting, color, and

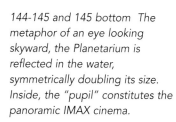

144-145 and 145 bottom The metaphor of an eye looking skyward, the Planetarium is reflected in the water, symmetrically doubling its size. Inside, the "pupil" constitutes the panoramic IMAX cinema.

144 bottom Motion, the leitmotif of Calatrava's works, is also evident in the Planetarium and the mobile structures of the entrance gates. The latter, like giant eyelids, regulate public access to the interior.

145 top Steel and glass underscore Calatrava's penchant for geometric precision. Special plates of glass were manufactured by Saint-Gobain Glass to meet the project's safety and strength requirements.

movement make it possible to create an exceptional show and infinite special effects to illustrate astronomic phenomena, with the aid of 48 slide projectors, four video projectors and a high-tech sound system.

The lower floor houses a colonnade formed by cement arches that support the roof, with ticket offices, a restaurant, and other services.

In 2000 the linear sequence from west to east was completed with the construction of the Museo de las Ciencias Príncipe Felipe, a large rectangular building (over 700 feet long) formed by the repetition of cross-section modules.

As impressive as the great expos of the 19th century, the science museum is a point of contact between past and future.

The southern side of the building displays its sculptural quality in white concrete, while the glazed northern façade, which resembles a frozen waterfall, offers glimpses of the five enormous concrete pillars within, which branch upwards like trees to support the stairs and elevators to the upper stories.

The interior features a long exhibition hall illustrating the evolution of life and the latest conquests in the field of science and technology, all based on an interactive

display philosophy that goes beyond the static model of the museum as a place for the collection of objects. The three stories illustrate three great themes in which the spectator actively participates, following the suggested itinerary. This is the largest center of its kind in Spain. It collaborates closely with the world's leading museums, and its consultants include seven Nobel laureates.

The Umbracle was built a year later, parallel to the museum but on a higher level. It offers visitors a view of the entire complex and allows them to enjoy the spectacle of the gardens reflected in the surrounding pools. The 1050-foot-long structure, formed by the

repetition of 55 white metal arches, is a contemporary reinterpretation of the "winter garden" and houses 50 different species of local flowers, as well as several trees. The kaleidoscopic effects are popular with visitors, who can also enjoy the open-air gallery that displays sculptures by contemporary artists along its path. The lower level offers indoor parking for cars and buses.

The last work to be built was the Palacio de las Artes, which completes the complex; it was inaugurated on October 8, 2005. It is a unique structure that makes an enormous contribution to Valencia's added cultural value, as it is equipped with excellent facilities to host all kinds

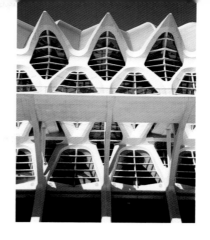

The City of Arts and Sciences

146-147 Depending on which side is observed, the Museo de las Ciencias Príncipe Felipe evokes different and contrasting images: the past, interpreted through the skeleton of an enormous dinosaur, and the present, with an ultramodern undulating façade composed of 4000 laminated-glass windows resembling a crystal waterfall. These aesthetic concepts were adopted in response to the strong sunlight typical of these latitudes.

147 top The module, which seems to revive the aesthetics of Gothic architecture, is repeated obsessively along the 790-foot façade of the museum.

147 center and bottom All the buildings in the complex are completely surrounded by water, symbolizing the sea – an environment that is examined and detailed inside – and evoking the historic memory of the site.

of international opera and great musical events.

Beneath the spectacular suspended roof, 755 feet long and 230 feet high, two symmetrical concrete shells house an auditorium that can seat 1300 people and can be adapted to stage operas, concerts and ballets; a 400-seat hall for chamber music, theater and other performances; and a 2000-seat open-air auditorium, protected by a roof and offering a spectacular view over the entire complex. Thanks to the use of the very latest technologies, it is a tribute to the dynamism of forms and functions, and, will surely become a hub of theater, opera, and music circuits. (Marco Tagliatori)

The City of Arts and Sciences

148 and 148-149 A modern reinterpretation of the winter garden, the Umbracle was built on a higher level than the rest of the complex. It has a panoramic promenade on the upper level, and car and bus parking on the lower level. This is the best vantage point for a splendid view of the entire complex. Its 55 white metal arches, which are 60 feet tall, beckon visitors to stop for a moment – out of the scorching Mediterranean sun – to observe the 50 different species of local plants, palm trees, and orange groves, and enjoy the open-air gallery displaying contemporary art.

149 bottom Many of the City's architectural motifs are a tribute to the Spanish architect Gaudì, whom Calatrava profoundly admires. His reinterpretation of natural forms closely approaches the work of the Catalan architect. Moreover, like Gaudì, Calatrava became a virtual overnight success because the forms of his works can be grasped so readily. The use of mosaics, created with Valencia's typical ceramic tiles, to finish the surfaces is also a constant stylistic element that links the works of the two architects.

150 and 151 center The buildings seem to glow at night, like suggestive and disconcerting architectural objects. The decision to build the structures using only white concrete negates textural differences and emphasizes their abstract and symbolic unity. Calatrava, who was a sculptor before turning to architecture, uses his buildings to introduce the general public to a different spatial and artistic experience.

151 top The Oceanogràfic boasts a highly varied program of activities, from study opportunities and illustrations of the problems of marine ecosystems, to the shows put on by Europe's largest dolphinarium.

151 bottom The buildings are reflected in the artificial pools around them, magnifying them to a monumental scale and accentuating their organic and figurative significance.

The City of Arts and Sciences

Casa de Retiro Espiritual

SEVILLE, SPAIN

Overlooking the Seville countryside, the Casa de Retiro Espiritual ("House of Spiritual Respite") is a little masterpiece of abstraction that probes the infinite tactile and expressive possibilities of architecture as a symbol. Functional reduction is highly intellectualized and has been taken to extremes here – to the utmost symbolic reduction.

Two soaring white walls set at a right angle to each other allude to a courtyard – a very common feature in this area – whose corner projects towards a fourth dimension. This emphasizes the subtle elegance of this attempt to assimilate and transform historical givens (the courtyard, the gate, the entrance). Virtually compressed, they are compelled to express

themselves through imprints, culminating with the overhang of the intricately carved wooden balcony that effectively concludes the entire composition. Two steep staircases emphasize the meaning of these paths and balance the composition from the interior.

History and meaning are interwoven in this semantic reduction. The only formal concession is an element resembling a perforated frame at the top of the structure that, in a certain way, filters the solid "lightness" of the white walls starkly outlined against the olive grove.

Ambasz deftly eliminated all superstructures in this "place of reflection" by using a device he has often repeated since then: he has "rooted" the functional layout, which is embedded within the simple geometric perimeter of a square.

The house becomes a symbol and manifests itself in the dazzling whiteness of two walls that, like beacons, signal a presence, a place, simply by encircling a space. It bears no resemblance to anything familiar – neither to Frank Lloyd Wright's Romeo and Juliet Windmill, nor to Philip Johnson's private white "thinking place," where somewhat traditional elements, i.e. physically concluded and elevated spaces, recur and allude to "normal" sequential construction.

The dream house materializes by dematerializing, assigning to this sublime interplay, represented by the metaphor of the walls, a psychological depth that is also far removed from John Hejduk's extraordinary and eloquent studies on the relationship between walls and space. But Hejduk's exercises were prototypes and tactical systems to explore the theme of residence, drawn from the pictorial roots of the twentieth century. They were essentially played out in the rapport between the wall or slab and the functional elements set

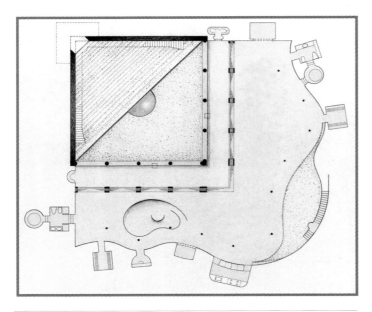

152 top and 153 top The layout of the area underscores the divergence between the "artificial," represented by geometry, and the "natural," represented by the landscape.

The stark geometric lines of the plan view are softened by the sinuous ones of the light well and the skylights, detailed in the top photograph showing the elements that relate to and mediate with the exterior.

DESIGN	CONSTRUCTION	DIMENSIONS	USE
E. Ambasz	1975	Usable area 3018 square ft	Residence

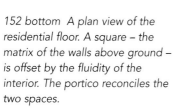

152 bottom A plan view of the residential floor. A square – the matrix of the walls above ground – is offset by the fluidity of the interior. The portico reconciles the two spaces.

152-153 Home and the outside world are two related yet contrasting spheres: this idea is conveyed through color, composition and eloquent vertical lines.

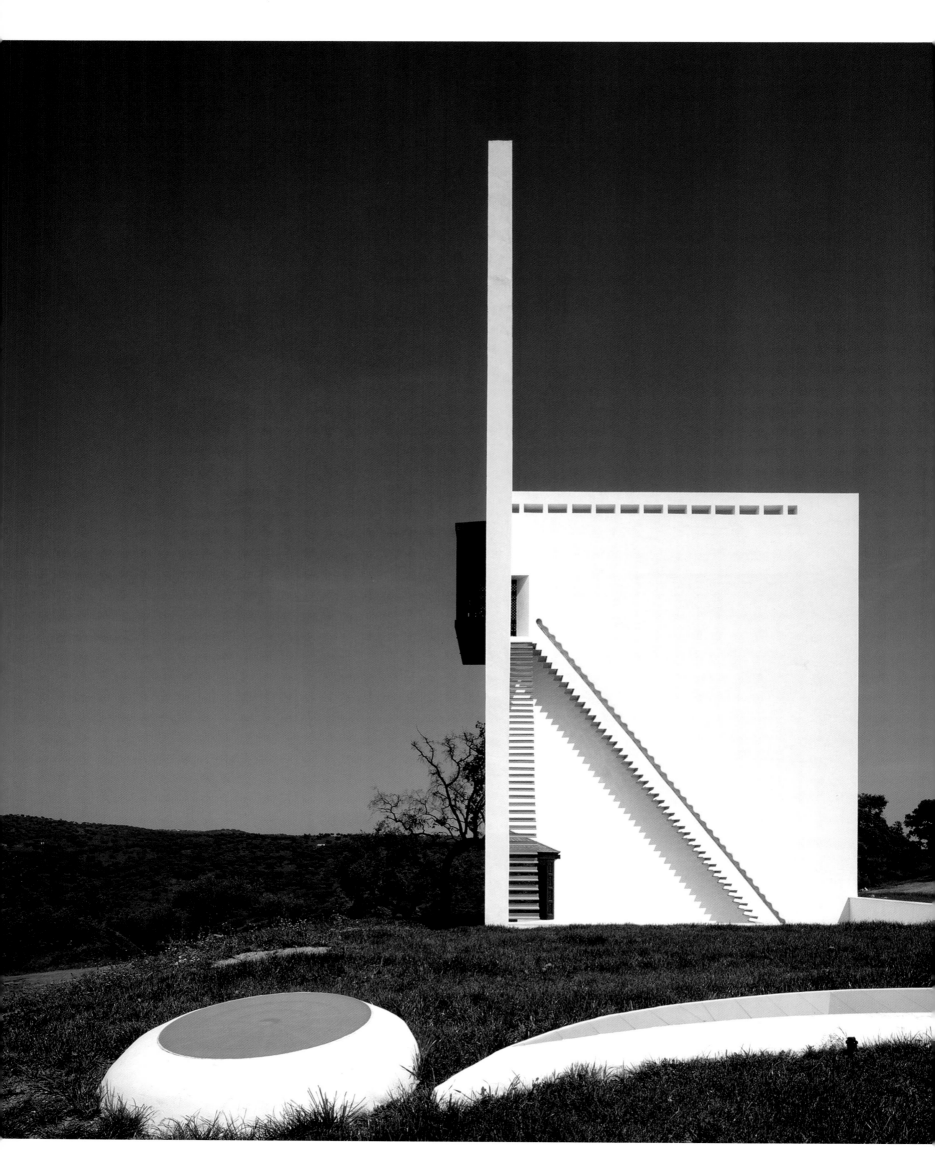

154

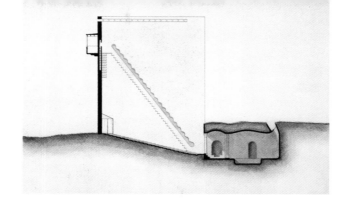

beyond it, in an astonishing balance of horizontal and vertical, slashes and inserts, perforation and solid undulating walls.

With Ambasz, the residential part is a sheltered place to be protected in every way, from the weather as well as the infiltration of water. The interior seems to be indifferent to any symbiotic or contextual relationship with the structure's natural surroundings, as revealed by the materials that are used, the

gleaming floors and the slits of the windows. The only intermediary between exterior and interior space is a gallery with its impressive and intricately carved trabeation.

The context of this architecture derives from its relationship with nature. "Modernism" is thus brought underground, making no concessions to organic details: it is the task of the white periscope outside to signal this. (Silvio Cassarà)

154-155 The obliteration of perspective magnifies the verticality of the wall slabs, creating unexpected atmospheres.

155 top The cross section shows the floors and living areas.

155 center and bottom These two photographs demonstrate how a space that is unfinished – and merely evoked – can create different emotional and psychological moods. What is evident in the first one (center) is the allusion to a private area that

is essentially protected by the view of the porticoed courtyard, juxtaposed with the walls rising above the ground. In the second one (bottom photograph) the corner wedge and the wooden rooftop terrace have dramatic expressive power.

156-157 The external approach to the building, in which the rapport between earth and sky is direct and immediate, creates surrealistic images that call to mind the works of Man Ray and Magritte.

E. AMBASZ

158 These extraordinary pictures show the interior in all its stark simplicity, emphasizing the transition from the interior (underground) to the exterior via an elevated portico.

158-159 and 159 top and center The lighting set in the false ceiling, the splendor of the flooring and the slender columns, coupled with the lack of any furnishings, dispel the notion that these rooms are underground, preserving the characteristics and finishes distinctive of an apartment. This architecture shuns camouflage – only to step in with a coup de théâtre.

159 bottom As this picture shows, the architect emphasizes that nature and the outdoors create effects that cannot be replaced by furnishing or décor. In effect, the intricately molded and exquisitely Spanish framework around the "void" – the threshold between the private void and open space, which is projected against the branches of a natural element, the tree, and is accessed via an ultramodern flight of steps – perfectly reflects the philosophy of the entire composition.

Casa de Retiro Espiritual

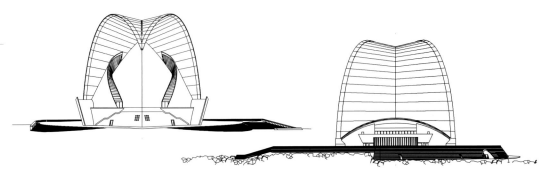

160 top Like an enormous sculpture, the Opera House takes up natural and organic forms. This is clearly visible in the symmetrical shell that encloses and protects the auditorium, the nucleus of the structure.

S. CALATRAVA

Tenerife Opera House

SANTA CRUZ DE TENERIFE, SPAIN

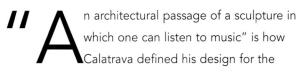

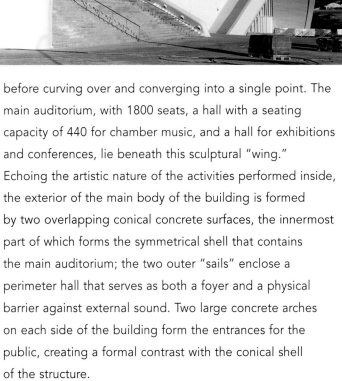

"An architectural passage of a sculpture in which one can listen to music" is how Calatrava defined his design for the Tenerife Opera House at its inauguration in September 2003. Built on a promontory next to the waterfront in Santa Cruz de Tenerife, in the Canary Islands, the building is the focal point of a larger redevelopment scheme for an area west of the city formerly occupied by industrial premises and an oil refinery, which are now being replaced by a vast public area with an alternating sequence of plazas and gardens that emphasize the great natural importance of the site.

The Opera House fits into this natural setting perfectly, evoking a gigantic wave about to break on the shore, and it is yet another artistic gesture of this prolific Spanish architect.

Constructed entirely from concrete – the only material feasible – the building is characterized by a dramatic freestanding roof that rises almost 200 feet from the base

before curving over and converging into a single point. The main auditorium, with 1800 seats, a hall with a seating capacity of 440 for chamber music, and a hall for exhibitions and conferences, lie beneath this sculptural "wing." Echoing the artistic nature of the activities performed inside, the exterior of the main body of the building is formed by two overlapping conical concrete surfaces, the innermost part of which forms the symmetrical shell that contains the main auditorium; the two outer "sails" enclose a perimeter hall that serves as both a foyer and a physical barrier against external sound. Two large concrete arches on each side of the building form the entrances for the public, creating a formal contrast with the conical shell of the structure.

On the exterior, much of the concrete is inlaid with shards of ceramic tiles, a traditional southern Spanish material, to create a white reflective surface.

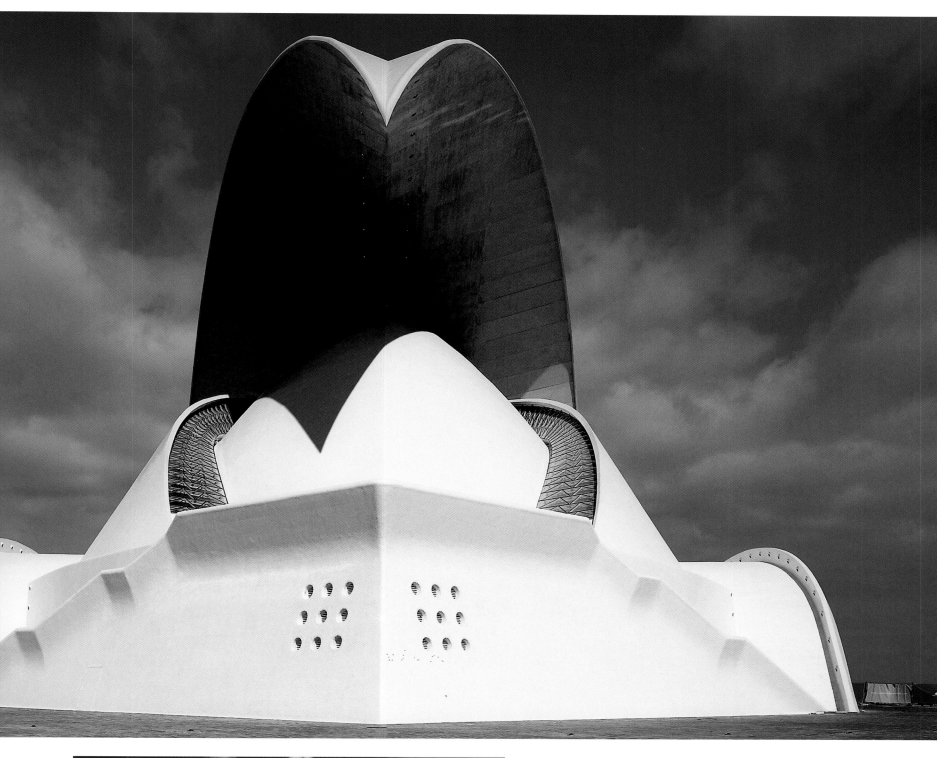

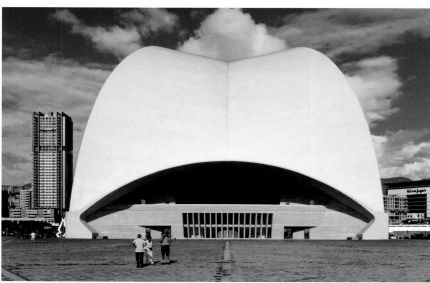

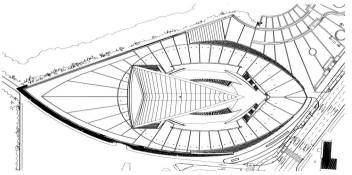

DESIGN	CONSTRUCTION	DIMENSIONS	USE
S. Calatrava	1990-2003	Total area 72,118 square ft	Auditorium

160 bottom and 160-161 A special crane had to be brought by sea in order to construct the auditorium, made entirely of concrete. The crane was used to assemble the precast elements – weighing 66 tons each – that form the structure of the wave, which rises to a height of 190 feet.

161 bottom left Visitors cross terraced squares and gardens to reach the building's main entrance.

161 bottom right The enormous central volume visible in the plan view is the element that generates the entire building.

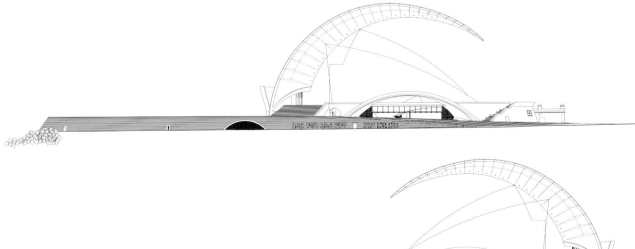

162-163 This dramatically three-dimensional and sculptural design concept affirms Calatrava's ability to challenge and overcome the basic principles of conventional architecture. The building, built on an area of nearly 260,000 square feet, is partly finished with crushed white ceramic tiles that reflect light, enhancing the powerful symbolism of this icon.

Tenerife Opera House

162 bottom Calatrava's drawings clearly show the subtle lines of force that determine the statics of the structure.

163 The sea counterbalances the white wave that looks as if it is about to break on the shore. The auditorium is destined to become a symbol of the revival, and the cultural and environmental development of a derelict industrial area that was occupied exclusively by depots and refineries until only recently.

The highly artistic exterior is matched by the technological sophistication of the interior. In-depth studies, performed on both 1:10 scale models and the building itself with laser surveyors, enabled the construction of cutting-edge overhead acoustic reflectors, whose task is to modify specific sound conditions and adapt the setting to a wide range of situations. Made of layered wood and fiberglass, the reflectors can open and close to reveal one of two finishes, depending on the type of acoustics desired in the hall. The dramatic effect of the design of the concert hall is heightened by the vaults created by the acoustic reflectors that cover the ceiling of the auditorium.

Critics have accused Calatrava of having created a "selfish" work of architecture, due to the solely sculptural purpose of the colossal roof that challenges the traditional canons of architecture, and pushing them – and the inevitable costs (nearly 75 million dollars) – to the limits of sustainability. Nonetheless, his clients showed enthusiasm and foresight, unflaggingly backing the project during the design and construction stages, which spanned a decade.

Consequently, to use Manuel Blasco's words, Calatrava "is an extraordinary creator of monuments who links his works to the environment, transforming the image of the world in which we live, making it his own and our own, and creating the spaces of a new age and the icons of our society."
(Marco Tagliatori)

Tenerife Opera House

164 top and bottom The "core" that holds the main auditorium, with 1800 seats, and a hall with a seating capacity of 400 for chamber music and plays, represent the heart of the building. All the service facilities are located in the area that forms the base of the enormous wing.

164 center and 165 The chamber music hall and the auditorium are equipped with high-tech mobile acoustic reflectors that make it possible to configure the space and adapt it to meet the different acoustical needs of various music genres.

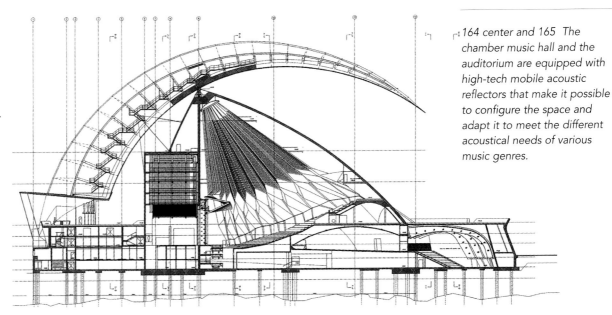

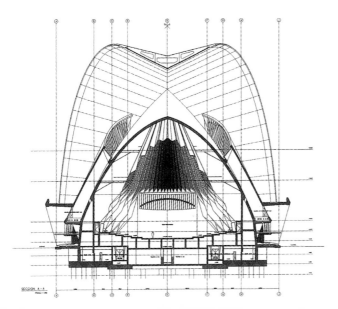

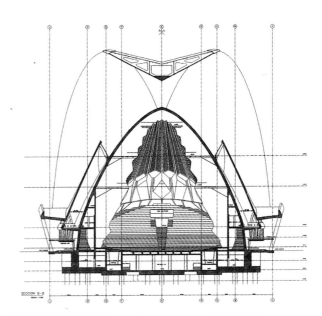

166-167 and 166 bottom The research center of the Nardini distillery was built by the family, which commissioned Massimiliano Fuksas to create a tangible link between the company's priceless legacy of the past and the high-tech dream of the future. Function, communication and style are conveyed in spectacular natural surroundings.

167 Light and airy glazed surfaces mark the vertical paths that link the underground space to the two glass ellipsoids or bubbles. The plans allude to the distillation process used to make grappa, and the structure designed by Fuksas is the symbolic alembic that transforms raw material into the finished product.

DESIGN	CONSTRUCTION	DIMENSIONS	USE
M. FUKSAS	2001-2004	TOTAL AREA 107,369 SQUARE FT	RESEARCH LABORATORIES, MULTIMEDIA CENTER

Nardini Event and Research Space
BASSANO DEL GRAPPA, ITALY

I n 2004, the old Palladian Bridge over the Brenta, long the symbol of Bassano del Grappa and the unmistakable logo of Distilleria Nardini, was flanked by the futuristic structure designed by the architect Massimiliano Fuksas and commissioned by the Nardini family, which has produced grappa for 225 years. Fuksas fully understood and embraced Giuseppe Nardini's ambition of "projecting the company into the future of the third millennium," in the hope of leaving a mark in the company's history. Nardini had two requests: the architect was asked to respect the trees in the park, designed in 1981 by Pietro Porcinai, one of Italy's leading landscape artists, and to create an underground auditorium to accommodate the 1500 visitors

that flock to the distillery every month.

Fuksas fulfilled these planning requests as the response to a natural need of the site. This "aesthetic edifice" – marked by uncompromising design – fully respects its setting, serving as an access to the ancient temple of Bassano Aquavitae that, in the unbridled imagination of the Roman architect, is the emblem of the distillation process.

Two worlds, two dimensions: a suspended one composed of two staggered ellipsoid glass bubbles, balanced on slender steel legs and housing the laboratories of the research center; a submerged one, a space carved into the ground to house a 100-seat auditorium. On ground level, a descending ramp leads to the auditorium, and it can also be used as an outdoor performance

Nardini Event and Research Space

168 top The laboratories are reflected in a pool that is just 2 inches deep, but the mirrored images of make the water look much deeper.

168 bottom The bubbles represent two different realms, contrasting the airiness of the research laboratories with the excavated 100-seat auditorium built to accommodate the 1500 visitors the company receives *every month. The main support for the structure is the diagonal elevator that, like the faceted concrete partitions of the underground floors, required extensive calculations and enormous effort to complete.*

169 Fuksas' attention to the environmental impact of buildings takes top priority in all his works, and it is tangibly transposed into both aesthetics and plant engineering.

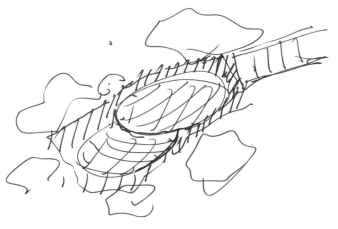

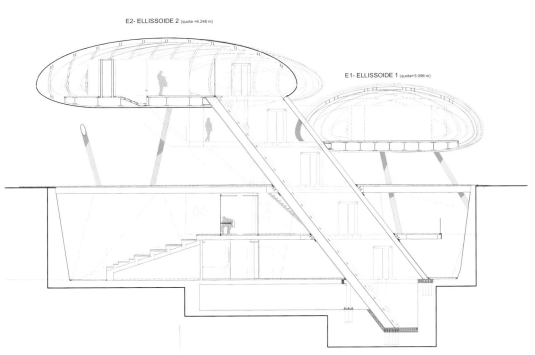

E2- ELLISSOIDE 2 (quota +6.246 m)

E1- ELLISSOIDE 1 (quota+3.096 m)

Nardini Event and Research Space

170 and 171 top For the exterior as well as the furnishings, great attention was paid to texture and surface treatment. The simple rooms reflect light and color.

171 bottom The main entrance is a "savage" space, carved into the earth, that seems to release energy, propelling visitors upwards towards the glass bubbles of the laboratories. The

underwater skylights, embedded in the pool of water above them, filter sunlight to illuminate the interior, taking up the sense of liquidity that permeates the entire design concept.

stage. The tension generated by the two symbols vanishes in the pool on the lawn, which reflects the bubbles above and filters sunlight into the auditorium through underwater skylights, creating a shimmering space that forges yet another link between the structure and its natural surroundings.

This eloquent image is reinforced by the diagonal structure of the elevator that, like the slender columns, does not seem to support the buildings but instead anchors them to the ground. It is the abstract representation of the transmutation of matter – distillation – and of the heaviness of the soil, but it also symbolizes the volatility of alcohol.

The leitmotifs here are transparency and sculptural lightness – and plenty of technology. The elliptical form of the two domes made it necessary to curve every sheet of glass individually (special laminated glass that meets top performance requirements was used). The underground area

reveals the great engineering feat involved in the static calculations of the structure, where concrete, steel and I-beams create supports and counterweights. Its construction called for highly specialized labor. Another interesting solution was adopted for the heating and air-conditioning system, distinguished by low energy consumption and zero emissions, which exploits groundwater that is heated or cooled by a thermal system.

The futuristic and technologically evocative design continues inside the bubbles with their furnishings. For example, the bathrooms feature glassy green materials, and the backlighting of the mirrors forms "fluid" images. In the lowest bubble, which houses the analysis laboratory, three long steel counters reflect the spectacular view of the Montegrappa mountain chain and the hillsides of Bassano. (Marco Tagliatori)

The New Exhibition Center

MILAN, ITALY

Pragmatic, experimental, possible: these words sum up the architecture of Massimiliano Fuksas. His is architecture that underscores the concept of an elevated construction's potential for existence and use.

This approach is un-Italian in some respects: for example, in the seemingly lighthearted use of color and materials, but also in the passion for a structural lack of sequence that is uncommon in the country's architecture. All these elements generate a process that we could define as the decomposition of the entire classic path – if one indeed exists – towards perfecting the architectural approach. This can yield results that may be discontinuous in form but that adhere to the principle of experimentation. History is "now" in this architecture. There are no formal icons or previously acquired repertoires from which to draw. This is a curious construction of anything that can lend meaning to space, and that can act as the forerunner and promoter of radically modern settings. It holds no traces of compromise, nor does it recover tradition, as anticipated by one of his early works, the Paliano Gym, with its unique concrete façade frozen in a simulated collapse. If anything, the architect's signature can be perceived in his ongoing confrontation with the other gravity: expansion of the structural layout to banish the inexpressive monotony of predictable immobility and of undifferentiated grids. This is demonstrated by the Ferrari Building in Maranello and, before that, by the building in Bordeaux with defined structures elevated to several stories. Lately, however, he seems to show a marked preference for clear materials, the kind that permit exploration and forays into fluctuating overhead structures, giving function to even the most ethereal and changeable element imaginable. This is the element that Le Corbusier doodled at the edge of some of his drawings, that Diller and Scofidio created by misting the water of Lake Neuchatel, and that, in Rome, we find in the EUR Congress Center, enclosed – naturally – in a clear shell: a cloud. Transparency over transparency, the defined and the undefined, matter and dematerialization are the areas in which Fuksas works, without conflict and without Magrittian allusions to different meanings. Utopia is elsewhere, not here. The EUR Auditorium anticipates the leitmotif of the strategy later perfected

172 Aerial sequences and details reveal an exhibition complex that unites the peripheral areas with the center through an uninterrupted line. The complex boasts a rational plan distinguished by only a few forceful elements.

173 The roofing of the pavilions is designed to channel light inside and transform the enormous skylights into fragments of landscapes with indistinct contours: craters and knolls that look as if they arose spontaneously.

DESIGN	CONSTRUCTION	DIMENSIONS	USE
M. FUKSAS	2002-2005	TOTAL AREA 8,072,933 SQUARE FT	FAIR PAVILIONS, OFFICES, RECEPTION AREAS, CONGRESS CENTER, SERVICE CENTER, MEETING ROOMS

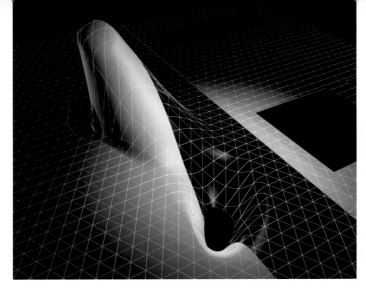

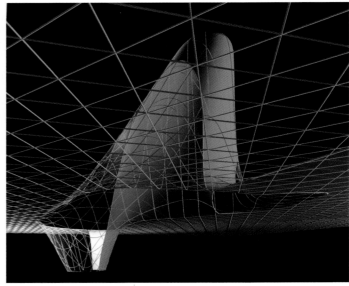

The New Exhibition Center

174 The essentially open gallery bears witness to the creation of seamless forms in the computerized rendering. This grid permits variety and modulations that are undefined

unless anchored to the ground – and to the idea that this path strives to convey and the spatiality it attempts to achieve. What is evident here is the architect's search for

complete transparency in the intangibility and lightness of the support system, designed to make the long elevated band as ethereal as possible.

175 Massimiliano Fuksas' sketches, in which the solemnity of black on white is livened by splashes of red, convey a compelling sense of naturalism.

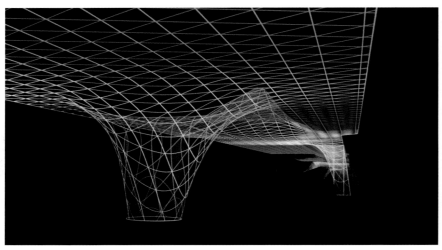

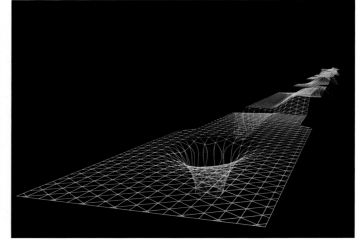

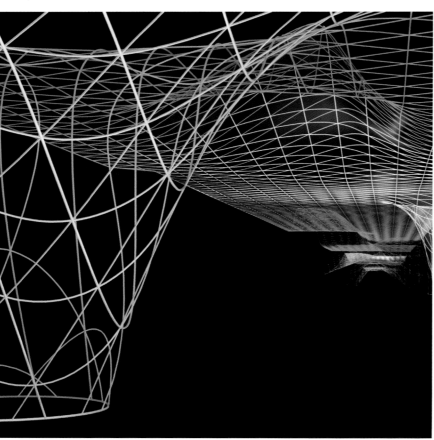

for the sprawling spaces of Fuksas' new exhibition center at the Milan Trade Fair Complex, where – in sheer size – the same assumptions discover a unique opportunity for study. On the one hand, they convey the impact that computers have had on design, while on the other they exploit them to define the contours of the indefinable. In essence, the indefinable finds its greatest expressiveness in a system of architecture that, wherever possible, assimilates transparency and dissolves it in a biological and artificial landscape of craters, implosions, undulations and, above all, linguistic continuity: identified continuity. The enormous mesh that unites the fabric of the central axis through a system of different glass triangles strives to merge into a single layout – and language – the functional differences between the exhibition areas and the service areas, yet it also emphasizes their diversity. The craters thus become the sources of natural light for the pavilions, arranged in a logical sequence. Elsewhere, however, they are also collection points for rainwater, swathed in the long wave that covers but does not enclose, protecting and channeling traffic in an interior / exterior extending for a length that would be difficult to handle with other devices. This is the system that

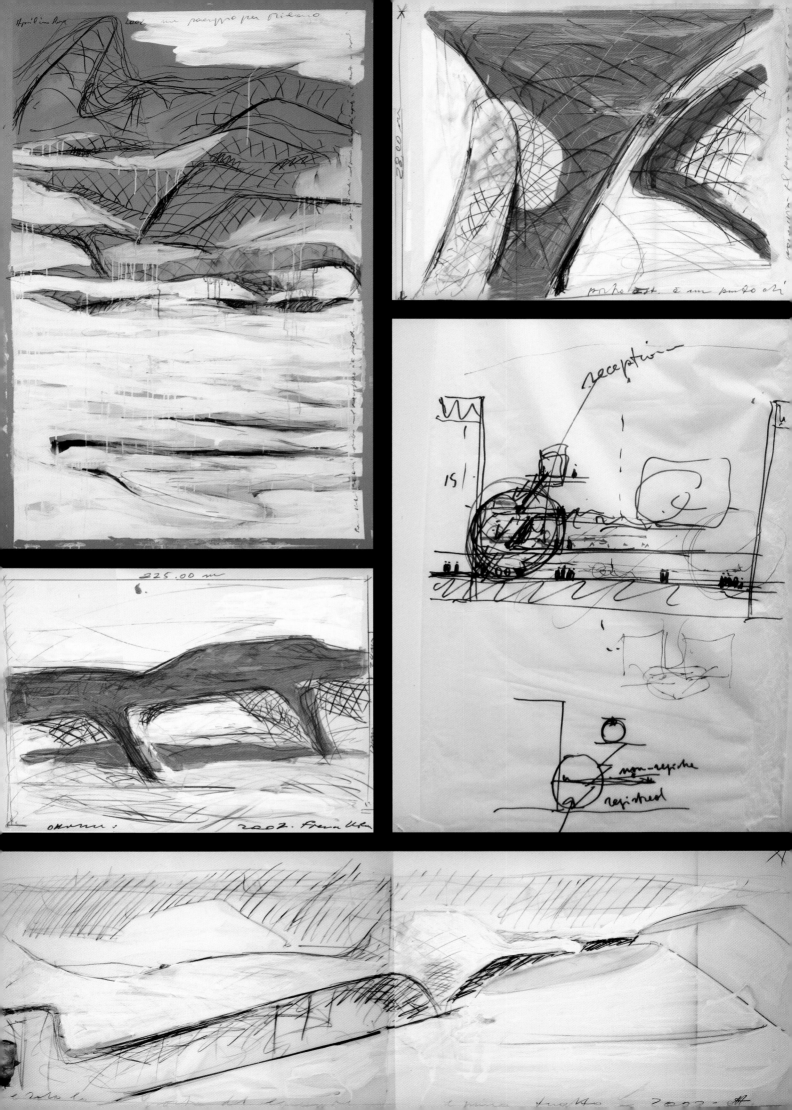

The New Exhibition Center

176 top The picture details one of the connections – also devoid of intermediate supports – between bodies, decisive traditional forms set close to an overhead structure.

176 center, bottom and 177 bottom The picture and cross section render the idea of an architecture that is present but that can be expanded to become an almost natural covering, like a finely structured gossamer web.

176-177 Two architectural elements – conceptualizing both implosion and the molten explosion of the structure – penetrate the edges of buildings with defined volumes.

architecturally and visually identifies the trade fair complex, but it also serves as the "roofing" for the routes between the pavilions. It is an intricate web that, as is the case at EUR, contains other small constructions: service areas, eateries, rest areas, and information desks. The concept of one of solids in voids, and of voids between the solids of the pavilions. They are shards of something infinite and changeable, like the society this "something" represents, without defining it but instead emphasizing some of its traits – with enormous optimism. (Silvio Cassarà)

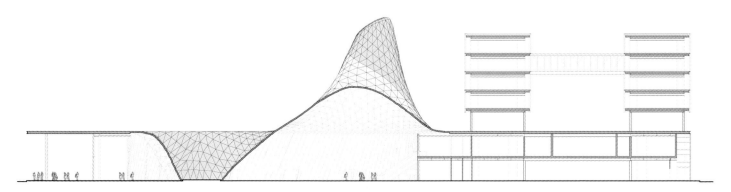

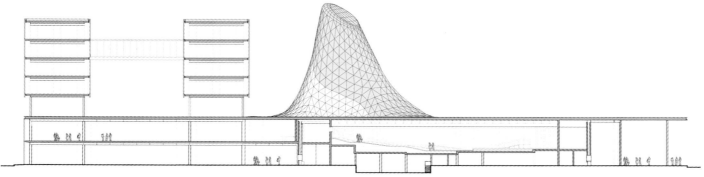

The New Exhibition Center

178 and 179 top An extraordinary view of the frustum-shaped section of the web, connected with the landing of the escalators of the internal transit areas, demonstrates transparency that takes up the triangulation system. This concept makes it possible to create surprising openings and intriguing views. As hinted at in the sketches, red is used here as the leitmotif that connects the various interior spaces.

179 center In the pavilions, the eye of light is connected to the tie rods of the structural web of the covering over the paths, alternating the repetitive continuity of the roof and creating a new elevated landscape.

179 bottom This side seems to reinterpret the view of Le Corbusier's Chandigarh Parliament, creating a sort of historicist bond that both the materials and function of the complex ostensibly ignored.

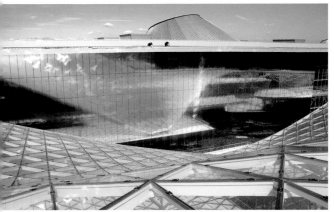

180 top, 180-181 and 181 bottom The unpredictability of the structure that sinks – only to emerge from the ground – is dramatic and intriguing. The device for collecting rainwater creates an extremely varied appearance, but above all it eliminates the need for gutters or any other element evoking vaguely traditional construction techniques. This design offers perspectives with an odd sense organic unity: for example, in the support systems of the structure. Above all, however, it relies on expressive uniformity that bows to the usual principle of adopting a triangular structural grid where possible, weaving a spell of transparency that marks this work's main expressive feature.

180 center and bottom Concavities, spheres, the glimmer of light on reflective material, three-dimensional spaces sustained by slender twisted columns in a seemingly unsteady balance: this corner embodies Massimiliano Fuksas' philosophy, brought to the scale of minimum intervention and the elaboration of complexity.

The New Exhibition Center

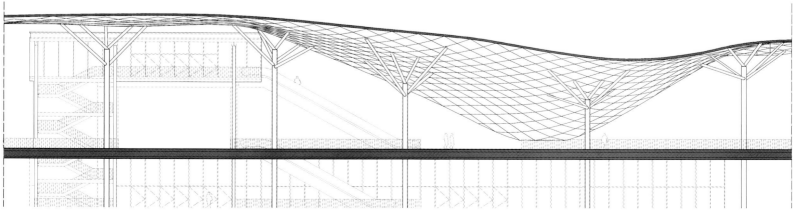

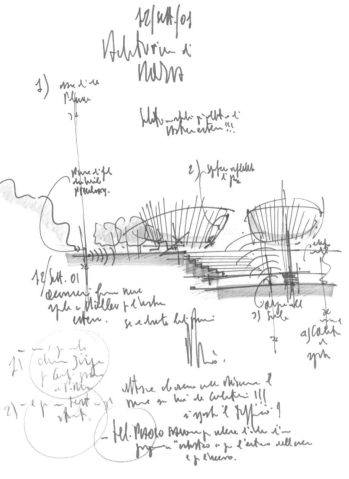

Auditorium Parco della Musica

ROME, ITALY

Designed by Renzo Piano, Rome's Auditorium Parco della Musica ("Park of Music Auditorium"), is situated behind the Parioli hillside, between the Olympic Village and the Flaminio district. It was designed as a 7.4-acre urban park planted with holm oaks, lindens and cypresses, and it features three separate music halls that can respectively seat 750, 1200, and 2700 people. The three curvilinear buildings are identical gems surrounded by greenery, and they are symmetrically set around the open-air amphitheatre that serves as a fourth auditorium. They are connected by a ring-shaped foyer that also leads to the museum of musical instruments, the dressing rooms and the archaeological site of the marvelous villa dating back to the 6th century BC, which was discovered during construction. The materials used in the park were borrowed from the traditions of ancient Rome: travertine and red brick for the faces and outside walls, wood for the roof joists and the interiors, and the lead of Renaissance and Baroque

182 top and bottom Even in the early planning stage, Renzo Piano's study sketch conveys the main elements of the built architecture: the rapport with park extending from the Parioli hillside, and the rounded concert halls set above the tiers of the outdoor theater.

182-183 The carapace shape that encloses the interior space was created by overlaying individual "shields" and curved "bodies", generating a subtle shadow line that runs through all the shells.

183 bottom The cavea is faced with slabs of Roman travertine and the retaining walls are made of brick. The auditorium has several levels: the cavea leads to the foyer and then up to the concert halls.

DESIGN	CONSTRUCTION	DIMENSIONS	USE
R. PIANO	1994-2002	TOTAL AREA 914,932 SQUARE FT	AUDITORIUM

domes to clad the new complex's three "music boxes," as Piano himself has dubbed his theaters, which are contemporary marvels that complement the capital's historical monuments.

The intriguing carapace-like forms designing the rhythmical structures of the auditorium were defined through a lengthy process of using scale models to check and simulate sound, and how it reverberates. This was conducted with the assistance of physicists and sound technicians to achieve the perfect and calculated propagation of musical notes. As a result, from the outside the three halls are identical in form, though different in size, in proportion to their seating capacity. Inside, however, the spatial outline changes according to the musical genre to be performed, responding to changing needs.

The small one is designed for experimental music, jazz and

freely – without necessarily attending shows and concerts. It is essentially another city district next to the center of Rome. With this work, Piano has continued his research into the architecture of music venues, which started with the IRCAM Center in Paris (1988–1990) and includes the concert hall at the Lingotto in Turin (1983–1995), the Kulturforum in Berlin (1992–2000), and the recent Paganini Auditorium in Parma (1997–2001), which was created by renovating a derelict sugar factory. Piano's philosophy conceives space as a shrine for listening, using the same approach with which one would carve an instrument used to create a specific sound. In both form and material, Piano has thus oriented his choices to achieve the kind of cherry sound box of the finest Stradivarius – but on an architectural scale. (Matteo Agnoletto)

rock, operas, and operettas. The medium one is more flexible, as the size of choruses and orchestras – as well as the position of the audience – can be varied by mounting mobile walls and stages, making it ideal for both symphonic and chamber music. The large one, with the intriguing vineyard seating arrangement around the stage, merging audience and performers, is the emblematic linchpin of the Auditorium, and this is where concerts for large orchestras, concerted works, and sacred and contemporary works are staged.

The Auditorium has been developed as a comprehensive music center, complete with a rich array of other services: stores, bookshops, cafés, bars, restaurants and recording rooms. All the areas are connected by a network of paths, walkways, porticoes and plazas where visitors can rendezvous

184 and 184-185 The foyer leads to the three concert halls, the service areas and the museum of musical instruments. In the large hall with vineyard seating terraces, which can accommodate 2700 people, the audience encircles the orchestra stage.

185 bottom left The photograph illustrates the exterior fire escape, protected by an overhang supported by steel struts that branch out from spherical joints.

Auditorium Parco della Musica

185 bottom right Travertine was used for the interior, whereas brickwork was chosen for the transit and service areas. Cherrywood was used to finish the concert halls. Piano's attention to construction details, coupled with the intriguing juxtaposition of materials, has created arrestingly elegant architecture that virtually becomes part of the history of Rome, representing an element of continuity.

Church of Dio Padre Misericordioso

ROME, ITALY

The Church of Dio Padre Misericordioso, which is commonly referred to as the Jubilee Church, was built outside central Rome after an invited competition intended to celebrate the Jubilee Year 2000.

The competition theme was inordinately complex for several reasons, such as the limitations imposed by the building lot. More importantly, however, the architect was expected to tackle a well-established genre, while also developing an area marked by undifferentiated urban sprawl in order to give it a cosmopolitan air. New York architect

compelling geometric lines, which make it immediately identifiable even from a distance, and the lack of color – virtually everything is white – it has an extraordinary emotional and physical impact on its surroundings.

In effect, the building is the "foreign" body needed to redeem the banality of the standardized appearance of the new residential complexes.

It is the alien that uses only a few materials – concrete and glass – to fine-tune a mechanism whose sphere of influence seems to overcome the objective limitations of its own

Richard Meier's proposal successfully addressed these needs. The compact structure is situated at the end of a slight rise, on a somewhat triangular lot in the residential district of Tor Tre Teste. It is almost completely surrounded by the types of buildings that represent the new cityscape of much of suburban Italy.

The church is powerfully rooted to the ground. With its

dimension to act as a visual catalyst and point of congregation.

Meier experimented with the use of a very Italian material: cement specially blended with white marble aggregates. He then continued his research into the expressive potential of "intelligent" forms for which, in other situations, he generally used metal structures and enameled metal cladding panels: strictly white, of course. Here, white goes beyond chromatic

DESIGN	CONSTRUCTION	DIMENSIONS	USE
R. Meier	1996-2003	Total area 15,069 square ft	Church

186 top This aerial view of the complex clearly shows the platform where the structure was erected, as well as the separation between the liturgical space beneath the "sails" and the parochial area distinguished by the bell tower.

186 bottom The enormous "sails" of the south façade of the church, made of reinforced concrete blended with white marble aggregates, were built using a specially designed metal framework that made it possible to exploit a constant radius of curvature, despite the fact that the sails differ in height. The grid etched on the surfaces plays a significant role in terms of architectural definition, conceptually connecting the building to the metal cladding panels the architect has often used in his other works.

186-187 The east façade is composed of a sequence of vertical sculptural elements: solids and partitions. The glazing establishes continuity between the separate parts, and it is clear that the overall composition effectively eliminates the solidity of masonry.

188 *This extraordinary picture shows the entrance with the sequence of graduated sails, stabilized by the enormous masonry "blade" – also curved – that establishes the structure's compositional balance. The curved lines of the elevated structures take up their horizontal outline, i.e. the arcs of a circle.*

189 left *This view of the altar clearly shows the compositional device of the sails and the difficulty involved in constructing them. The sails have openings in the middle, forming graduated doorways. The outermost sail seems to graze the ground, letting a shaft of light in through the floor-level opening.*

189 right *The entrance and a sculptural composition house the organ. The picture shows the sequence of vertical elements that define the spaces, connected by the partitions of the glazed roof, in which the uprights play a fundamental visual and compositional role.*

Church of Padre Misericordioso

meaning, establishing a link with specific aspects of architectural historiography. The building plies forms that are simple and precise, yet stately. Three enormous curved elements, generated by the circumference of the layout of the complex, enclose the liturgical spaces. Instead, the secular areas such as the pastor's residence, the recreation center and the parish offices face each other along the interior courtyard, which is a level down from the entrance. These white "sails" – perhaps the mnemonic remains of enormous classical and Roman vaults, the fragments of spaces that are somehow familiar to us – mark (yet do not enclose) the spaces of a church that effectively has no roof other than the changeable skies, visible through the glass connecting the sections. Three curved symbols and a slab mark the two-dimensional conclusion of the façade, with a sense of transparency that alludes to volumetric spaces, which are not expressed physically but have nevertheless been created.

And there is light. Yet it is not the "guided" light of Sant'Andrea al Quirinale that, penetrating and precise, streams through the oculus of the dome.

It is not the management of Baroque darkness, nor the reflected brilliance of the white dome of Borromini's San Carlo alle Quattro Fontane. The Jubilee Church is a space constructed through light: light that inundates and expands the curvilinear surfaces in sequence and carves out the separate body of the altar, in a purist, modernist sculptural exercise applied to liturgical functions. This sculptural effect characterizes the parochial area and alludes to the hallmarks of Meier's approach to residential and museum architecture. The distinction between the two is clear and, if anything, the design method is more intricate than unusual. It goes beyond the forms of tradition and the visual formal repertory that the architect nonetheless considers intrinsically valid. The church effectively purifies well-defined geometric forms – circumferences – that seem to rotate on the horizontal plane and come to a halt without completing an entire turn. The result is ideological and real continuity between horizontal and vertical, interior and exterior. It merges structure and architecture, taking up the construction tradition of some of the world's greatest religious buildings. (Silvio Cassarà)

Bibliotheca Alexandrina

ALEXANDRIA, EGYPT

During the 3rd century BC, Alexandria was the site of the largest cultural institution of antiquity, the legendary Library of Alexandria, which housed all the knowledge of the Western world. A third of the building's 700,000 books were destroyed when Julius Caesar's troops set it on fire, and the Christians burned the remainder in AD 392.

Today, over 1500 years later, Alexandria is once again home to a library that is the repository of contemporary knowledge. The Bibliotheca Alexandrina ("Alexadrine Library") is a project that represents man's wish to enshrine

his desire to learn: a place of memory and communication.

The Egyptian government and UNESCO jointly promoted the construction of the Middle East's most important international study and research center in Egypt's second-largest city to make it a focal point for culture, education and science.

The building, designed by Christoph Kapeller of the Norwegian firm Snøhetta, was conceived as an open space, supported by a tall and slender colonnade that separates the rooms and is reminiscent of ancient temples.

The designer's main aim was not to create a historic or futuristic building, but a timeless one to represent the heritage of human culture. The new library was built over the ashes of the old one, in the city's Brucheion Quarter , a historic area that was also home to the museum and the royal palace of the Ptolemaic

190 top and 190-191 The façade, created with over 75,000 square yards of stone, is a cyclopean sculptural surface. It is composed of 6.5-foot-tall stone blocks, and the various alphabetical and symbolic forms known to man in every era have been carved on it. Every possible form of communication has been sculpted on this granite surface, from mathematical language to Braille, musical notation and barcodes.

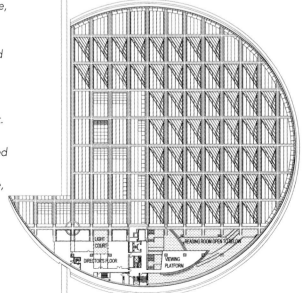

DESIGN	CONSTRUCTION	DIMENSIONS	USE
C. KAPELLAR	1995-2002	TOTAL AREA 861,113 SQUARE FT	LIBRARY

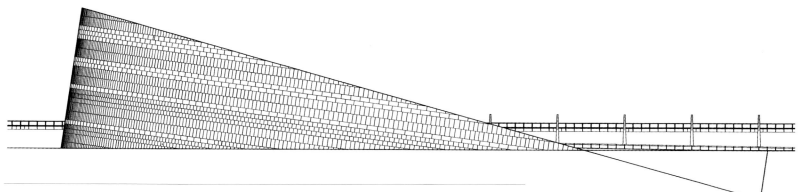

190 center The disk, set at a 16-degree angle, is punctuated by partitions, calling to mind a gigantic microchip rising from the sea and reaching towards the heavens. Material and technology eloquently come together here.

190 bottom The round roof, shown in the vertical section, is an element that links the memory of the past, represented by the curved face, with a focus on the future.

191 bottom The cylinder, set at a 16-degree angle, rises to a height of 122 feet and extends 52 feet into the ground. The structure is crossed by a straight line, a pedestrian bridge linking the city university.

Bibliotheca Alexandrina

192-193 The stone flooring creates a contrast with the pool, which has been planted with papyruses and local vegetation that act as a natural system to clean and filter the water.

192 bottom left The planetarium is an enormous sphere with a diameter of nearly 60 feet; the exterior is divided into wedges. Suspended above the garden, it symbolizes the image of the Earth seen from the Moon.

192 bottom right The broad public square was designed to give the complex an area where people can stop for a quiet break, but also it also connects the different areas and encourages users to socialize.

193 The library assets count books donated by numerous countries, including Italy. Priceless ancient books are safeguarded in the library alongside digital texts.

dynasty, just a few yards from the Mediterranean shore.

Today the legend of antiquity has been revived in a project with many different meanings: a disk that faces the sea and is partly submerged, like the rising sun of ancient Egypt.

The main feature of the new library is its cylindrical structure diagonally sliced at a 16° angle, topped by a circular roof covered with square glass panels. This structure intentionally evokes a microchip and acts as an adjustable screen to control the amount of light in the reading room throughout the year.

The diagonal of the roof rises to the seventh story, creating a vast interior space marked by nearly 100 concrete columns with stylized capitals recalling the Egyptian lotus.

The cylinder measures 525 feet across; the structure is embedded to a depth of 52 feet, rising to 121 feet above

books and creating the sensation of a giant amphitheater.

This large space houses two museums, a conference center that can accommodate thousands of people, halls for temporary exhibitions and the world's largest reading room. The 3000 workstations, including 300 computerized ones, cover an area of 215,000 square feet, with wooden floors constructed using Norwegian materials and techniques, in which cultures mingle to create a space that recalls the National Library in Paris, but with the atmosphere of a mosque.

The interior of the reading room develops a new concept of library space, using overlapping balconies to house the collection of eight million books, audiovisual resources, materials for children, young people and the disabled, and the complete Internet archive. The building also houses other cultural activities, such as a workshop for the restoration of

street level, and is enclosed by a wall of large granite panels from the Aswan quarries.

The stone is incised with scripts in all alphabets – the symbols invented by man to communicate – ranging from hieroglyphs to alphanumeric characters, musical notation, and computer and genetic codes.

The roof is supported by the imposing curved wall, whose exterior becomes an enclosure supported by slender columns and illuminated at the base by diffuse lighting. The interior space, 525 feet across and 263 feet high, is divided into 14 mezzanines, allowing users to move among the collection of

manuscripts, research centers for areas ranging from manuscripts to writing, calligraphy, information sciences, studies on Alexandria, the Mediterranean and art, and a planetarium with an interactive Exploratorium for children.

The planetarium is a sixty-foot sphere suspended above a concave garden, inspired by the first image of Earth as seen from the moon. A large public square connects the main entrance of the library with the existing conference center and the city via a bridge from the university campus. This makes it a crossroads while preserving its status as a place of silence and contemplation. (Guya Elisabetta Rosso)

194 top The Burj Al Arab, built on an artificial island about 920 feet from the shore, resembles an unfurled sail, and has become the spectacular icon of the new Dubai. The image of the tower, which houses the only 7-star hotel in the world, has rapidly become the symbol of the United Arab Emirates.

194 bottom The tower is connected to the mainland by a causeway, which physically separates the structure from its surroundings and ensures the privacy of hotel guests. The main façade, which also serves as structural reinforcement, resembles a billowing sail in the middle of the blue waters of the Persian Gulf.

Burj Al-Arab
DUBAI, UNITED ARAB EMIRATES

Dubai's Burj Al-Arab, a luxury hotel owned by the Jumeirah International chain, has become the icon of this Middle Eastern city. Soaring to a height of 1053 feet, it is an internationally unique example of this type of building.

The hotel, which has been awarded seven stars for its superb quality, was commissioned in 1993 and took five years to complete. The architect Tom Wills-Wright decided to build this monumental work on an artificial island in order to emphasize its symbolism and heighten the extraordinary impression of an enormous billowing sail on the blue waters of the Persian Gulf.

The hotel can be reached via a 918-foot causeway that links the island to the shore, and at night the causeway is lit up to create a dazzling kaleidoscope. This entrance is off limits to casual visitors, guaranteeing the privacy of hotel guests. The hotel can also be reached by helicopter, landing at the heliport cantilevered from the 28th floor.

The complexity involved in constructing this marvel of engineering is evident in sheer numbers: the bearing structure of the building is distributed over more than 86,000 cubic yards of concrete and more than 9900 tons of steel.

The main structural reinforcement is constituted by the curtain wall, 860,000 square feet of glass covered by a double-knit Teflon fabric skin that looks white during the day but reflects all the colors of the rainbow at dusk, creating a dramatic light show. The glazed surface has a maximum width of 180 feet and rises to a height of

DESIGN	CONSTRUCTION	DIMENSIONS	USE
T. WILLS-WRIGHT	1994-1999	TOTAL AREA 344,445 SQUARE FT	HOTEL, RESTAURANT, CONFERENCE ROOMS, FITNESS CLUB

195 Twilight is the perfect time to observe the changing nuances of the façade, which is transformed from dazzling white during the daytime to a shimmering iris in the evening, creating a dramatic kaleidoscope of colors.

196 top This aerial view facing the mainland shows the exterior of the steel-and-concrete bearing structure. It is composed of the large vertical element that soars to a height of over 1000 feet, with a panoramic suspended restaurant and two ribs that support the horizontal and diagonal members.

196 bottom and 197 The building's support structure is composed of an exoskeleton made of concrete and steel that can withstand winds of up to 280 mph. The girders are anchored to the curved ribs and held in place by steel truss rods.

Burj Al-Arab

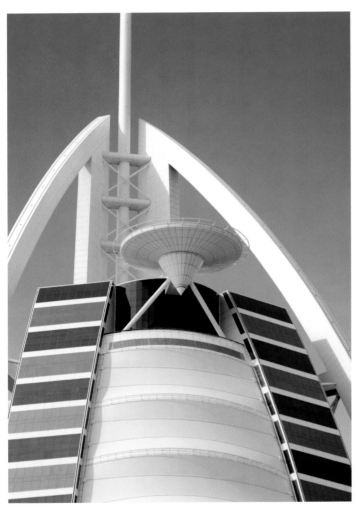

675 feet, reflecting 70% of the light and heat from the outside. In calculating structural load resistance, the wind speed for vertical loading was estimated at 218 mph, increased by an extra safety factor so that the building can withstand winds of up to 280 mph.

Inside the hotel, lavishness and pure elegance have been combined with breathtaking results. Precious silk, Italian and Brazilian marble, and 22-karat gold fixtures create an extraordinary mélange of Arabian tradition, avant-garde design, and state-of-the-art technology. Just past the entrance, the lobby, created between the walls of an aquarium, occupies a third of the internal space and is dominated by the blue and gold hues of the enormous bombé columns. The atrium, which is 590 feet tall, could easily accommodate the Statue of Liberty, and every thirty minutes the fountain spurts 100-foot jets of water into the air.

The 202 suites, which boast from 1830 to 8400 square feet

of floor space, have enormous windows affording a stunning view of water, and the décor is elegant and sophisticated. Each floor has about ten rooms, whereas the Royal Suite covers the entire 25th floor, and has its own private elevator and movie theater.

There are common areas on virtually every floor of the hotel. The bar on the 27th floor offers guests an incomparable view of sunsets over the Persian Gulf. Alp Muntaha restaurant, at a height of 656 feet, is suspended over the sapphire sea and can be reached in just thirty seconds using the world's fastest elevator. The Al Iwan, whose décor reflects the most luxurious local tradition, is an area of enormous formal interest. Lastly, the sophisticated wellness center on the 18th floor, decorated with gilded mosaics inspired by the formal principles of the ancient civilizations of the Middle East, offers a marvelous view of the sea from the deck with the swimming pools. (Francesco Boccia)

Burj Al-Arab

198 The cavernous atrium leading to the upper levels, where the guest suites are located, is distinguished by enormous bombé columns finished in 22-karat gold. The atrium is nearly 600 feet tall and every 30 minutes the fountain on the ground floor shoots enormous jets of water into the air.

199 top left The Club Suite, which boasts 3500 square feet of floor space, is laid out on two levels and furnished in a Middle Eastern style.

199 top right The Assawan Spa & Health Club has gyms, swimming pools, a sauna, a hydromassage, a solarium, a squash court and a fitness room.

199 bottom right The Sahn Eddar, one of the cafés in the tower. Mosaics and marble in warm tones, coupled with modern furnishings, create a welcoming atmosphere. From the interior, guests can admire the top of the columns of water from the fountain on the ground floor.

199 bottom left The Al Muntaha restaurant, at a height of 656 feet above sea level, is accessed via an elevator that travels at a speed of 20 feet/second. Its enormous windows offer visitors a breathtaking view of the Persian Gulf. The restaurant, which can seat 120 people, serves European cuisine.

The Hong Kong and Shanghai Bank

HONG KONG, CHINA

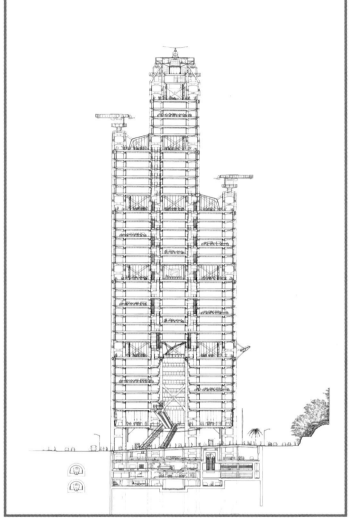

The Hong Kong and Shanghai Bank is situated in Hong Kong's Central District – the business complex on Victoria Island – in the old colonial city across the strait from the Kowloon Peninsula.

In 1978 an international competition was announced for the construction of the headquarters of the Hong Kong and Shanghai Bank, and the award went to Foster and Partners.

The firm doubled its efforts to satisfy the requests of its client, which wanted "the best bank building in the world" to flank the historic London premises with new ones in Hong Kong.

A process of consultation, which also involved a Feng Shui expert, established that the objective of the building was to express the function of the bank in its form.

This concentration of forces resulted in a structure that, at the time, was considered one of the most technologically advanced in Asia and, given its high cost (approximately 600 million dollars), undoubtedly also one of the most expensive.

It was clear from the start that the project was different and innovative with respect to the usual construction of tower buildings. Indeed, the traditional skyscraper structure built around a blind central core housing the transit areas was abandoned in favor of a design that shifted the circulation structures of the tower to make room for a "hollow" heart flooded with light.

The need to erect such a large structure in an existing built-up urban fabric called for the use of high-quality prefabricated and factory-finished modules. In order to ensure the highest qualitative standards, most of the components were prefabricated and subsequently assembled on site.

DESIGN	CONSTRUCTION	DIMENSIONS	USE
N. FOSTER	1979-1986	TOTAL AREA 1,065,627 SQUARE FT	HONG KONG AND SHANGHAI BANK OFFICES, PUBLIC SPACE

200 and 201 With the Hong Kong and Shanghai Bank, Foster developed his theory on the communicative language of bearing structures. The skeleton of the building is displayed to highlight the function of the building.

202 The suspension structure with asymmetrical lattice girders: the "short" part supports the service areas and fire escapes, whereas the "long" part sustains the floors.

203 top The structure is set on four massive supports, thus allowing the building to be "suspended" over a patio, creating a delightful environment that has become very popular.

203 bottom The bank donated this space to the city as a public area, in exchange for authorization to exceed the permitted building volume of the skyscraper. The curved glazed roof over the plaza is pierced by escalators set at an angle, which lead directly to the third floor of the building. Visitors can look upwards from the patio to see the interior of the bank.

Hong Kong and Shanghai Bank

Additionally, again due to the conformation of the site and the impossibility of using traditional construction techniques, the steel masts forming the structural frame of the building served as the shafts of eight cranes, which were used to erect the skyscraper and were left on its roof for maintenance purposes.

The result is a well-structured building, with a stepped profile composed of three juxtaposed towers that are respectively 36, 44, and 29 stories high, thus creating floors varying in width and depth, and forming garden terraces.

As mentioned earlier, the mast structure also allowed the service core to be pushed to the perimeter, making it possible to create deep-plan floors and a large column-free inner area, thereby permitting a highly flexible layout. This construction scheme has allowed the ground-level space to be very permeable towards the exterior. In fact, the square in front of the building passes beneath it, creating a covered pedestrian plaza that is perfectly integrated with the urban context. Indeed, this is a public space to all intents and purposes, donated to the city in return for authorization to exceed the permitted floor area ratio, which allowed a 20% increase in the overall built area.

Visitors can reach the atrium of the bank from the plaza by means of escalators that penetrate its glass floor. The spectacle that meets their eyes is completely unexpected: an atrium that rises to a height of 170 feet, equivalent to ten stories, which terminates in a computer-controlled mirrored "sunscoop" that filters and reflects sunlight down through the atrium and the glass floor to the plaza below.

The sensation of flexibility in the layout of spaces is reinforced by the use of mobile and generally transparent walls and by the sobriety of the paneling, ceilings, floors and furnishings, all carefully chosen from a color palette ranging from black to light gray, with a few touches of red recalling the Chinese chromatic tradition.

One of the main goals in constructing the building was to ensure the maximum versatility of the spaces over time. This objective has evidently been achieved, judging by the interior that is completely free of rigid elements that could have blocked it in a static situation. Furthermore, the stepped construction of the building allows the possibility of extension in the event that the floor area ratio is increased. The areas housing the infrastructures, ranging from the telecommunications network and air-conditioning system to

Hong Kong and Shanghai Bank

204 The escalators that start at the covered plaza lead to the bank offices. The glass floor of the atrium permits visual contact between the interior of the building and the area beneath. The offices are arranged around the 10-story atrium. The mirror system installed at the top of the atrium and the glass walls filter and reflect sunlight, illuminating the atrium and offices, as well as the glass-ceilinged plaza.

205 Other areas can be accessed from the five main floors via a complex series of stairwells that intersect with the bearing lattice girders, forming elements that follow and sinuously cross each other in a virtual snake dance.

the electrical wiring and IT cabling, are located beneath the lightweight paneled floors. This makes the systems easily accessible for maintenance and also allows them to be extended or upgraded with the latest technology.

Further proof of Foster's move away from the traditional conception of spatial layout is evident in the fact that the views inside the Hong Kong and Shanghai Bank are not limited to a single floor, as in traditional skyscrapers. Fast elevators serve the five main stories, and from here the building's occupants can reach their workspaces by means of groups of escalators that serve portions of the building composed of five or eight stories. This allows everyone, from office workers to executives, to perceive a much larger space, thus also conveying a far greater sense of belonging.

Although unconventional in form, the "best bank building in the world" is discreet. Indeed, while occupying a prime site on the extension of the pier that is the departure point for the ferry that crosses the strait to Kowloon, it nevertheless manages to characterize the decidedly varied urban landscape in which it stands without being obtrusive, as so often happens with eccentric or glittering modern skyscrapers.

This is also due to the building's subdued colors, such as gray, which is the main shade of both the structure and the external aluminum cladding.

The rounded form of the roof, the eye-catching vertical shafts and the imposing dimensions of the "bridges" that support the floors visually restore the building to the urban

Hong Kong and Shanghai Bank

scale. Indeed, it is only when the eye reaches the base, between the two lion guardians (Stephen and Stitt), that one actually realizes the impressiveness of the building, which is evident if one considers the 590-foot height of the main tower.

Foster has received numerous awards for the Hong Kong and Shanghai Bank, including the Premier Award of the Royal Academy of Arts and the 1986 Institution of Structural Engineers Special Award. (Alessandra Di Marco)

206 top Night view of the skyline of Hong Kong's financial district: on the left is the Bank of China Tower, with the Cheung Kong Center next to it; the Hong Kong and Shanghai Bank is on the right.

206 bottom The illuminated building reveals the five main floors, the additional horizontal division of space, the entrance to the covered plaza and the impressive vertical bearing structure.

207 The main faces of the building are characterized by enormous piers that support the bays, which in turn bear the weight of the floors. The massive piers stand out on the main façade.

208 top The subtropical climate, characterized by a high level of humidity, promotes the formation of clouds, which shroud the tower during most of the city's cold winter months and create the impression that the building is not anchored to the ground.

208 bottom The 101 Taipei Tower dwarfs the buildings around it, standing out as the city's majestic landmark. The Taipei Financial Center is composed of eight sections set on top of each other, making the skyscraper look even taller.

101 Taipei Tower

TAIPEI, REPUBLIC OF CHINA

I n the 20th century, the challenge of constructing the tallest building was battled on American soil, mainly between Chicago and New York. With the new millennium, Asian countries are clearly determined to push the United States and Europe out of the competition. The expression of economic and technological advancement, skyscrapers manifest the achievement of capitalistic development, marking a specific territory and attracting international attention.

Inaugurated on December 31, 2004, "101 Taipei Tower" is one of the tallest buildings in the world.

The debate over which building is the tallest on the planet revolves around the measurement methods that are applied.

Rising to a height of 1667 feet, 101 Taipei Tower surpasses the Petronas Twin Towers in Kuala Lumpur, which held the previous record. The tall antennas on both of these buildings contribute to their record-breaking status.

The building houses various functions, ranging from commercial activities on the lower floors to a fitness center, offices on the intermediate floors, three observation decks, and communication facilities on the top floors.

Two elevators that can reach a speed of over 3315 feet per minute have been installed to connect the various activities. The elevators have been studied from an aerodynamic standpoint and have been equipped with the most advanced safety systems on the market.

DESIGN	CONSTRUCTION	DIMENSIONS	USE
C.Y. LEE	1999-2004	TYPICAL FLOOR AREA: 4440 SQUARE FT	OFFICE, LIBRARY, EVENTS AREAS, RESTAURANT, SHOPS, FITNESS CENTER

209 Ru Yi, Chinese symbols that represent success and satisfaction, can be seen on the outside walls of each of the eight sections of the tower, in the form of stainless-steel sculptures that weigh 2.75 tons each.

101 Taipei Tower

210 The shops and businesses at the tower attract hordes of Taiwanese. The mall at the 101 Tower combines the appeal of shops with a central public area – Taipei City Square 101 – that replicates the oval pattern and two-color floor of Rome's Piazza del Campidoglio.

211 top A colossal gilded sphere weighing 805 tons, suspended from anchored steel cables, has been installed on top of the tower to buffer vibrations. In addition to its structural function, it is also a remarkable tourist attraction.

211 bottom left At the base of the tower, the 7-story building known as the Podium has an area of 156,000 square feet, with a shopping center and a venue where events are staged, forming the largest enclosed public space in Taiwan.

211 bottom right To plan many of the aspects related to the organization and design of the interior, the C.Y. Lee firm turned to an expert in Feng Shui, the Chinese art of maintaining the balance of energy in buildings.

The building underwent numerous variations due to restrictions imposed by the vicinity of the airport, but in the end it was possible to build it to the height that had initially been planned. Taking up the local cultural tradition was a point of pride in designing the building. As a result, the skyscraper is decorated with floral motifs and references to traditional Chinese symbols. The plans for the tower revolve around the number eight, considered a lucky number that brings prosperity and security.

The vertical element, composed of eight overlaid sections, rise from the base and flare upwards slightly, evoking the structure of bamboo shoots or – as some have prosaically

noted – the carryout boxes from a Chinese restaurant. The tower rises from the band around the top of the base, which is adorned with circular decorations representing a contemporary interpretation of ancient Chinese coins.

The steel-and-concrete construction marks a challenge not only in terms of the height that has been achieved, but also on a structural level. Built in a high-risk earthquake zone and subjected to the pressure of strong winds, which often turn into typhoons, the skyscraper is a complex feat of engineering. The flexibility of the primary structure is augmented by a device that makes it possible to damper the building's resonance to seismic vibrations, thus stabilizing it. The enormous suspended sphere that performs this function attracts countless tourists, who climb to the observation deck at the top of the tower.

Structural solidity is matched by layout flexibility to accommodate a variety of activities. Traditional commercial activities are flanked by a space designed as a gathering place for visitors. The flooring of the central "plaza" faithfully copies the oval pattern of Rome's Piazza del Campidoglio and offers the spectacle of the gallery that encircles it and rises to a height of 148 feet. The tower's distinctive features include the observation points at the 89th, 91st and 101st floors, which offer visitors a striking panorama that stretching from the mountains to the sea. (Guya Elisabetta Rosso)

212 left Traditional Chinese decorations give the metal framework a refined air. The steel structural members are set alongside glazed sections that illuminate the spaces below.

212 right A closer look at the support system for the skylight of the Podium reveals that the elements used to solve technological problems also serve a decorative purpose.

213 The long central skylight of the Podium, which covers an area of 28,900 square feet, is one of the largest in the world. The local culture powerfully influenced the decorative motifs, which have been interpreted in a high-tech style.

101 Taipei Tower

214 The linear forms of the vertical surfaces accentuate the skyscraper's grandeur. The Ru Yi motif is also taken up inside, forging a link between interior and exterior.

215 top The sleek décor of the rooms, done in light tones, contrasts the spaces in which bright colors have been used to accentuate different functions.

215 bottom left In addition to graceful floral motifs, geometric decorations give the interior a bold and dynamic character.

215 bottom right In some cases, the technological elements that decorate the walls are repeated serially, alluding to the concept of the technical reproducibility of artwork.

216-217 The form of the Sendai Mediatheque, by the Japanese architect Toyo Ito, originates as a single enormous glazed structure with a square plan, which is 165 feet long on each side. The building is about 122 feet high. The west side presents a galvanized steel structure covered with vertical louvers.

216 bottom The 13 shafts – the photograph shows one of the internal ones – look like tree roots or sea algae, and are composed of slender steel pipes.

217 left The "skin" of the building reflects the Japanese architect's desire to design a structure akin to an aquarium, in which the transparency of a thin glass partition ensures a constant visual rapport between interior and exterior.

217 right The glass panels cladding the building differ in opacity. This helps modulate the intensity of sunlight and forms decorative motifs on the façades. Natural light and a view of the outside help orient visitors and allow them to move about without the need for any signage.

DESIGN	CONSTRUCTION	DIMENSIONS	USE
T. Ito	1995-2001	Total area 161,459 square ft	Mediatheque, bookshop, exhibition galleries, offices, cinema

Sendai Mediatheque

SENDAI, JAPAN

For the Sendai Mediatheque, built in Sendai, Japan, between 1995 and 2001, Toyo Ito effectively followed the evolution of his own design philosophy, which led him from an architectural style inspired by the modernist movements to a minimalist type of development marked by the use of readily available material and research into new urban forms. Thus, the Japanese architect used a single parallelepiped structure to create continuous spaces separated by partitions that are barely perceptible.

The building plans are based on the presence of three separate formal and functional systems: horizontal division, achieved by creating six floor slabs, vertical elevation

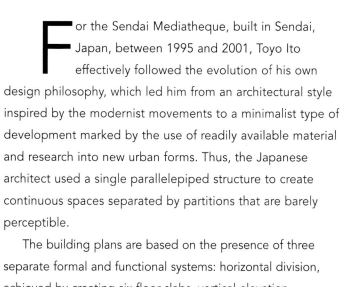

composed of thirteen ribbed shafts, and the cladding of the façades, effectively a "skin" separating interior from exterior.

The building has a square plan (165 feet per side) and is 122 feet tall. In Ito's words, in designing it he was "not concerned with formal expression" but strived to achieve something prototypical and essential.

The floor slabs, which are just a few inches thick, divide the building horizontally and seem to float at different heights without any connections visible from the outside. As a result, they sketch out uneven lines on the façades, without being bound to custom and convention.

The shafts, composed of tubular steel, serve several

purposes, acting not only as static support for the floor slabs but also for mobility and connections between the floors of the building via stairs and elevators. At the same time, they also serve visual and formal purposes, as these dematerializing wells bring sunlight from the roof to the ground floor, and they house utilities, cables and wiring.

The "skin" of the building reflects the idea of creating a building akin to an aquarium, in which it is always possible to maintain a visual rapport with the exterior and a constant sense of orientation. According to the architect, it is precisely the opposite of what happens in subway stations, in which one is forced to follow unnatural indications in order to move about. The four faces of the faces of the building are substantially

different. The main one is effectively a glass partition that alters the perception of the interior depending on the time of day, in an interplay of reflection and transparency. The internal floor slabs jut out from the east and north faces, accentuating the transition between the different bands designed on the façade, which is also clad with different materials, both clear and opaque. The west side has a translucent structure in galvanized steel covered with vertical louvers.

The main entrance leads to the double-height lobby, which has an information desk and a café. Part of the glazing on the south side can be opened completely, creating an intriguing effect of compenetration of interior and exterior.

Sendai Mediatheque

All the upper levels have a free floor plan – in deference to the teachings of Le Corbusier – and have been designed to ensure maximum flexibility and adaptability for different activities. The Shimin Library, exhibition galleries, and audiovisual mediatheque are located here, in addition to a meeting room, offices, a café, and a 180-seat cinema. The façades of the top floor of the mediatheque are completely glazed, offering a sweeping view of the city. (Francesco Boccia)

218-219 Each of the six intermediate levels of the Mediatheque was planned by a different designer. The photograph shows the interior of the ground floor, designed by Kazuyo Sejima. It houses the administrative offices, an information area and a cafeteria.

219 The space between the shafts and the "skin" highlights the design concept of the building: the floors seem to overcome the force of gravity and look like they are afloat in space. The vertical support elements, hollowed out and dematerialized, give the overall structure a sense of lightness.

Sendai Mediatheque

220 top The shafts channel light from the roof to the ground floor. The intermediate floors have been designed with a free layout, based on the principles of Western modernism and clearly alluding to the architecture of Le Corbusier, whose works profoundly influenced Ito on a cultural level.

220 bottom At night, artificial lighting from the interior transforms the appearance of the building: the sun's reflection in the windows is replaced by a clear view of the interior, creating spectacular forms and colors, and giving the shafts a distinctive nocturnal mystique.

221 At night, the Sendai Mediatheque clearly reveals the height differences of the individual floors, intentionally designed by the architect to avoid any references to conventional concepts or uniform rhythms, discernible as a sign of unwarranted expressive rigidity.

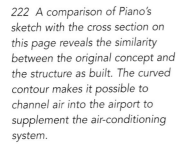

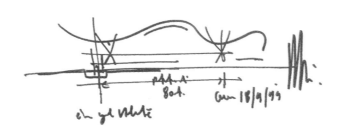

222 A comparison of Piano's sketch with the cross section on this page reveals the similarity between the original concept and the structure as built. The curved contour makes it possible to channel air into the airport to supplement the air-conditioning system.

223 The enormous roof was built using steel girders that are visible from both the interior and exterior, accentuating their characteristics and transforming them to the iconic element of the entire structure. The complex is clad with steel panels mounted in a thin layer.

Kansai International Airport

OSAKA, JAPAN

Among the masterpieces of history, we can trace a common thread that links the monuments of the past with the infrastructural, engineering and architectural works of modernity. From the Egyptian pyramids to cathedrals, and from bridges to dams, the size, the number of workmen required to build them, the iconic image embodied by the constructed works and the events involved in completing them pertain to the definition of the legend that makes certain human undertakings unique and extraordinary, handing them down to future generations as the symbol of the era that spawned them.

Kansai International Airport, inaugurated by the Emperor of Japan on June 27, 1994, is unquestionably one of the most extraordinary and impressive achievements of the 20th century. To complete this work, a team of Japan's best engineers created an artificial island in Osaka Bay, three miles

fact that, according to static calculations, the island will sink by over five feet. This slight – and expected – settlement is managed by a calibration system connected to hydraulic jacks, so that any excessive sinking will be blocked and each pile can be adjusted to the right position. This precise and meticulous approach was also applied in constructing the terminal building.

The unique form designed by Piano stems from studies on the dynamic flow of winds, used to created the sinuous, undulating shape of the airport. In cross section, the curved roof is the outcome of an additive series of arcs obtained from toroidal geometry, whose center is 10 miles below the Earth's surface, with a radius inclined at 68° with respect to the horizon. This gives the structure exceptional elastic capacity to withstand the impact of earthquakes, a common problem in Japan, as the building oscillates along the main axis. This essential precaution fully protected the airport

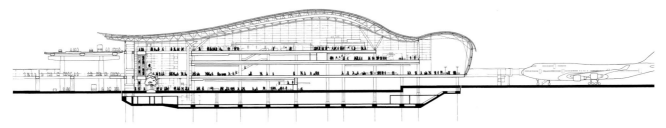

offshore, building it in just five years using fill. The takeoff and landing runways, and the airport terminal designed by Renzo Piano with the collaboration of the London engineering firm of Ove Arup, are located on the island. When the island was finished, the area of Japan increased by 5.8 square miles: in fact, this new atoll made it necessary to reprint atlases and maps.

The decision to build the airport at sea stemmed from the need to improve the population density of the country and from the lack of available land to accommodate such a large infrastructure. The island platform is anchored to the ocean floor by a thousand piles embedded into the subsoil through 65 feet of seawater and 65 of mud, into the very bowels of the earth in more than 130 feet of bedrock. Special sensors have been installed to monitor ground settling, due to the

DESIGN	CONSTRUCTION	DIMENSIONS	USE
R. PIANO	1988-1994	TOTAL AREA 4,693,065 SQUARE FT	INTERNATIONAL AIRPORT

during the earthquake of January 1995 that devastated Japan and razed Kobe, which is the same distance from the epicenter as Osaka.

The island and the terminal trembled when the earth shook, but not one window broke at the airport, underscoring the structure's safety. The computer-modeled mathematical matrix optimized the curvilinear profile of the roof based on the ocean breezes conveyed under the roof and exploited for natural cooling of the interior.

The application of a false ceiling, which only partially covers the roof girders, allows air to circulate from the "sky side" to

the "earth side" without requiring the installation of conduits or ducting. Air flows freely and stirs Susumu Shingu's mobiles, used by Piano to bear witness to air and wind. Indeed, the terminal forges a direct relationship with these two elements and is a new temple consecrated to them. In effect, the passenger terminal is a sophisticated air-conditioning and climatization device. In appearance, however, it resembles a glider that has just touched down. Its architecture is composed of the central service and entry area. The docking wings – with 42 gates – extend symmetrically on both sides.

The complex is one mile long: an enormous internal cavity with endless sightlines, filled with lush gardens and trees. Light streams in through full-length windows, illuminating the routes of this immense "air city" populated every day by 100,000 passengers in transit from around the world. To deal with this enormous longitudinal development, the plans turned to the visual devices used by the Greeks in

Enormous three-dimensional trusses made of 263-foot-long tubular steel sections, installed crosswise along the terminal, form the structural framework enclosed by the roofing, composed of 82,000 completely identical steel panels. The uniformity of this surface captures and reflects light, creating rich and sparkling shades of silver.

One of the hallmarks of the Kansai terminal is that the structure inside the building is visible, alluding to the Beaubourg, whose affinities are manifested in the intriguing concept of transforming the cross section into façade. In Paris and Osaka alike, the steel framework – orthogonal at the museum, curvilinear for the airport – serves as the end enclosure for the two buildings yet also as a cross section. This striking and extremely elegant touch of artistic genius minimizes and brings down to earth the high-tech exaggeration often mistakenly linked with Piano's sophisticated solutions.

the ancient temples to minimize optical deflection. The ends of the wings are tapered, varying depth perception and correcting for the disorientation caused by the idea of dispersion and boundlessness.

The construction technology used to build the complex in record time – just 4 years – to stay within the budget of 12.5 billion dollars was also subject to its layout and compositional aspects. The 6000 people who worked on it, responsible for completing this fascinating challenge, applied standardized technological processes using interchangeable parts, thereby ensuring optimum construction conditions.

The importance of the steel roof – the only architectonic sign that is virtually suspended midair, and also a "flying" element evident in Piano's detailed sketch summarizing his project – is magnified by the complete dematerialization of the dark glass walls.

This means that only the rooftop is visible at a distance, thus appearing to rise weightlessly from the ground, whereas the interior creates visual continuity with the sky and the horizon, underscoring Piano's desire to merge architecture and nature in his works. (Matteo Agnoletto)

Kansai International Airport

224 The entrance "canyon" of the airport covers several floors and is embellished with plants and trees. Just under the roof, the visible structural elements create a complex and dazzling spatial effect.

224-225 In this view of the waiting areas, the glass railing along the passenger concourse to the gates is visible on the left.

225 bottom The photographs convey the immense size of the airport, with the intriguing air diffusers installed to ventilate the boarding areas. Enormous glass walls let plenty of light into every corner of the airport. The steel trusses, the glazed façade and the furnishing modules designed by the Renzo Piano Building Workshop converge to define a coherent structure that is instantly recognizable.

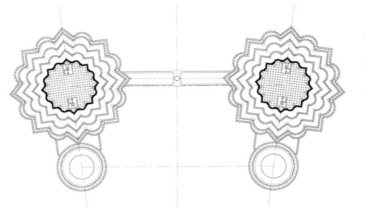

226 *The two overlaid squares rotated by 45° – the Islamic iconographic elements that generated the plan of the towers – define a circular grid composed of 16 piers forming the vertical bearing structure of each building. The lines of symmetry of the two towers converge slightly.*

227 *The outlines of the towers dominate the Kuala Lumpur skyline. The symbol of Malaysia's astonishing economic development in recent years, the complex of the Petronas Towers was designed to house big companies working in the advanced service sector, futuristic shopping and cultural centers, auditoriums and convention halls.*

Petronas Towers

KUALA LUMPUR, MALAYSIA

Between 1996 and 1998, the American architect Cesar Pelli designed and built the Petronas Towers in Kuala Lumpur, Malaysia. Commissioned by the Petronas Oil Company, the 88-story twin towers are serviced by 76 high-speed elevators and 30 escalators.

The towers, which are tapered towards the top, have nearly 3.7 million square feet of floor space and are almost 1500 feet

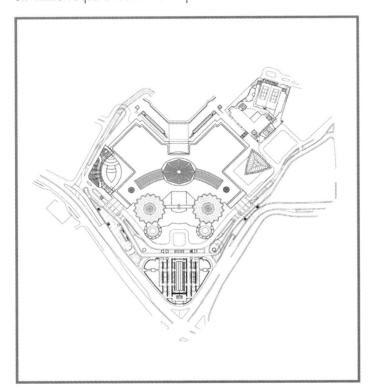

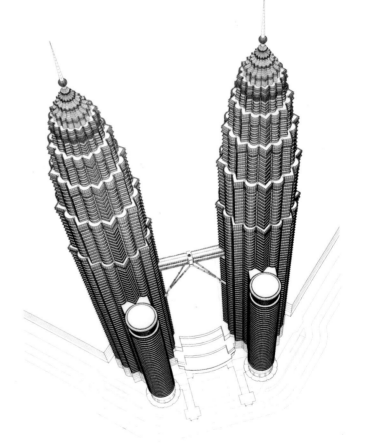

DESIGN	CONSTRUCTION	DIMENSIONS	USE
C. PELLI	1996-1998	TOTAL AREA 3,678,028 SQUARE FT	PETRONAS OFFICES, OTHER CORPORATE OFFICES, CONFERENCE CENTER, AUDITORIUM, LIBRARY

tall. They were designed as corporate headquarters. Their layout was determined using primitive geometric figures that were overlaid and turned by 45°, sketching out variable and discordant geometries that multiply in direct proportion to the height of the structure, reflecting the conceptual complexity of the building's design and alluding to our human difficulty in understanding the transcendent.

Two squares, which form the pattern that generated the plans, take up Islamic symbolism to represent the Earth and

the four cardinal points, though they are not the only cultural and iconographic references to Eastern traditions. In essence, they reflect the desire to generate a convergence between conserving the specificity of place and conscious openness towards a technological and globalized future. These concepts are mirrored not only in the perfect symmetry of the organism, which in some respects abandons the Western modernist

conception of similar structures, but also in the fundamental importance of the void between the skyscrapers. This void is broken up and emphasized by the Skybridge, which is nearly 200 feet long and weighs 825 tons. This pedestrian bridge, which serves as a formal connection between the towers and facilitates circulation, is set between the 41st and 42nd floors at a height of about 560 feet. At the same time, however, it also marks the upper conclusion of a clear barrier that opens up to the Malaysian sky: it is a bridge yet also a visual gateway to infinity.

Petronas Towers

228 Viewed from the side, the tapered outline of the tops of the towers and the two rods allude to the religious iconography of the temples of the forests of Thailand. The two rods add more than 230 feet to the height of the buildings.

229 top The shape of the Petronas Towers, which evokes Asian building traditions, contrasts the modern trend towards the loss of cultural identity in architecture, which has increasingly turned to globalized forms.

229 bottom The Petronas Towers pertain to the category of architectural works with a powerful emotional impact, making them a key figurative experience in the formal expression of the 20th century.

The location of the complex created technical problems that were difficult to solve. The tropical climate, characterized by the scorching sun and strong winds, made it necessary to use compatible materials and façade divisions, as well as static solutions that met the building's particular structural requirements.

The cladding of the exterior required 700,000 square feet of stainless-steel plates that reflect the sunlight, creating dramatic effects and nuances. The glazed parts, which called for 828,000 square feet of glass, were sized to reduce radiation in the

interior. The exterior projections that the architect has dubbed "tropical walls" serve as brise-soleils and effectively characterize the shape of the building.

From a static standpoint, system criticality – and this applies to any skyscraper – comes from oscillation triggered by natural events. To solve this problem, passive control devices, commonly referred to as tuned mass dampers, were used. They are composed of counterweights connected to the structure via a system of springs mounted in the parts of the structure that are subject to the greatest oscillation.

The Petronas Twin Towers were the world's tallest construction from 1999 to 2005, despite objections that the measurement of the height of the building was incorrect, as it included the two tall rods. The rods increase their height by more than 230 feet, making them higher than effectively taller structures. (Francesco Boccia)

230 top The supports of the Skybridge were designed to withstand the oscillation caused by the strong winds typical of tropical climates. The bridge, built based on the static principle of the hinged arch, is located at the 41st floor.

230 bottom The windowed Skybridge owes its fame to a spectacular scene from the movie Entrapment, starring Sean Connery and Catherine Zeta-Jones. The bridge linking the buildings is 192 feet long and weighs approximately 825 tons.

230-231 The Skybridge uses devices known as tuned mass dampers, with a system of springs and hydraulic dampers to counterbalance any vibrations.

231 bottom The bridge, set at a height of 558 feet, allows users to move from one tower to the other, and with the towers it forms a visual gateway.

232-233 and 233 The interior of the towers is organized with a circular layout around the elevator shafts. The loggias house shops and businesses and the elevators – 76 in all – move at a speed of 11.5 to 23 feet/second. In front of the entrance to the building, there is a plaza with a fountain.

234-235 The plans by architect Cesar Pelli were inspired by the country's cultural heritage, and they merge contemporary motifs with the stylistic elements of traditional Malaysian crafts, such as woodcarving and songket weaving. The façades, clad with plate glass and steel, are highlighted in this ant's-eye view.

Petronas Towers

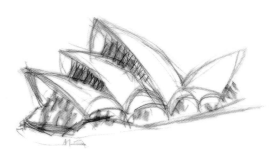

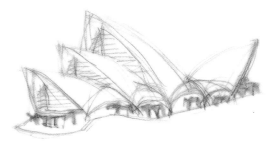

Sydney Opera House
SYDNEY, AUSTRALIA

Designed by the Danish architect Jørn Utzon, the Sydney Opera House is one of the world's greatest buildings. It created a new archetype among the formal expressions of the second half of the 20th century and has become the undisputed symbol of Australia. The Opera House stands on a 4.4-acre site next to Sydney Harbour. There is also an amusement park and the area is connected to the nearby Harbour Bridge. The building has become a favorite attraction even for tourists with no interest in opera, who flock to admire it.

The site was once the location of the Bennelong Point Tram Depot, which was opened in 1902 and demolished in 1958 in order to build the new theater.

The setting is spectacular: the building reaches out towards the sea, projecting the spirit of the city onto it and celebrating it to visitors arriving by ship – the same means first used to communicate with the rest of the world.

Indeed, the entire theater recalls this liquid element in the shiny, sculptural surfaces that the white building forms on a strip of land to connect the blue ocean sailed by the great explorers of the past with the brand-new world of Australia.

Chosen for its great evocative power and excellent design from over 230 projects submitted by international architects, the entire building is characterized by the form of its roof, inspired by nature. The surfaces reach out and curve towards the land and the sea, opening in a fan of new directions that contrast with and complement the vertical lines of the nearby city.

The building was constructed between 1959 and 1973, overcoming countless structural difficulties and intense technical, political and economic conflicts.

The initial enthusiasm for a work presented as a decidedly new and unclassifiable structure – and whose great originality was immediately acknowledged – was followed by a number of perplexities due to the formal and structural complexity of the design. These doubts were backed by what was presumed to be the limited experience and skill of a young architect who was just 38 years old at the time of the competition.

236 top The poetic and soaring lightness of this architectural work was evident even in the earliest design phases. It has been compared to ocean waves about to break on the shore, an imaginary crustacean and the billowing sails of a ship.

236-237 The view of the Sydney Opera House from the sea welcomes visitors and flaunts the splendid overlapping sails that form its roof, glazing and plinth, the compositional elements that helped Utzon win first prize in the competition to design the concert hall.

DESIGN	CONSTRUCTION	DIMENSIONS	USE
J. UTZON	1959-1973	TOTAL AREA 484,376 SQUARE FT	AUDITORIUM, THEATER, RESTAURANT

237 top The square leading to the Opera House, with the "Guillaume at Bennelong" restaurant and the tip of the roof over the main structure, which houses the Concert Hall. The lines of the shell are the outcome of the simplification of an extremely complex design process, which was required to achieve the right balance between construction requirements and expressiveness.

237 center An aerial view of the Australian landmark, set on a promontory, shows the compelling compositional harmony and complex geometric forms that have made it the very icon of Sydney: Utzon's Opera House is an extraordinary monument.

237 bottom The general layout of the Opera House, designed by the Danish architect Jørn Utzon: the staircase leading to the foyer and the two buildings housing the Opera Theatre and Concert Hall. The fanlike arrangement of the space embraces the architect's work, offering it to the sea.

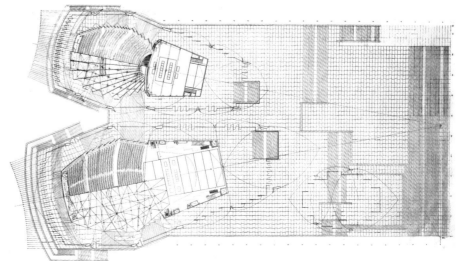

238-239 *The sea offers the best vantage point for viewing the Opera House. It took years of research – during which it seemed that construction would ultimately be impossible – to arrive at the structural solution of building the roof in thousands of precast elements.*

238 bottom *The west view of the building shows the outline of the roof, the plinth and the entrance to the foyer. The curvature of the sails was designed by circumscribing them in a sphere with a diameter of 246 feet, making it possible to precast the required elements.*

239 top *Nagata Acoustics, the company that worked on Frank O. Gehry's new Walt Disney Concert Hall, was commissioned to conduct studies to improve the acoustics of the Concert Hall. World-famous orchestra conductors such as Edo de Waart and Gianluigi Gelmetti were also consulted.*

239 bottom *Like almost the entire interior of the Opera House, the Concert Hall was not the work of Utzon, who designed only the exterior, but that of a team of Australian designers that completed its construction in 1973, over a quarter of a century after the international competition.*

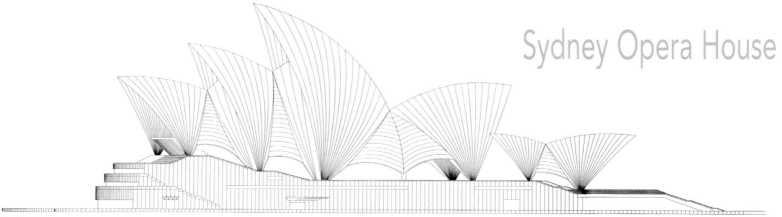

Sydney Opera House

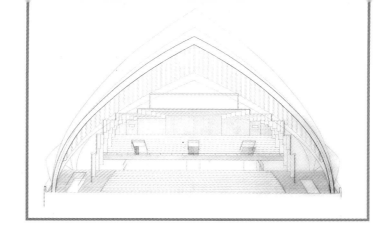

Consequently the British engineer Ove Arup, already renowned as an expert in similar buildings, was appointed as structural advisor for the project. As construction proceeded, the structural solution for creating the enormous shells of the "fifth façade," as Utzon called it, never emerged. For four years, hypotheses for the construction of the shells failed to yield the hoped-for results and there seemed to be no way of reconciling the original design with static requirements and available construction technology.

In the fall of 1961, however, Utzon himself came up with the solution to the problem, in the form of a method based on a rigid geometric system. He derived all the individual elements of the roof from the surface of a single sphere with a 246-foot radius that – in an extreme simplification of the infinite possible parameters – was broken down into 2914 precast concrete

models them to form a single expressive desire, aimed at achieving a static and structural solution that has become a powerful compositional language.

Utzon resigned during construction, before he had the chance to complete the interiors and windows, which were designed and created by a team of Australian designers using 66,700 square feet of glass. However, the Sydney Opera House should really be considered incomplete in relation to the intentions of its original designers. The only parts that can be attributed to the Danish architect are the sails of the roof and the plinth, which was changed in respect to the initial design. Nonetheless, such a distinctive feature makes the building immediately recognizable. Indeed, this was the destiny of Utzon's sails from the outset, for they became the very icon of Australia within just a few decades. All subsequent departures

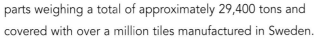

parts weighing a total of approximately 29,400 tons and covered with over a million tiles manufactured in Sweden.

Utzon removed all overlays to express the underlying concept and essence of his creation: the generating principle hidden until then, but demonstrated clearly and perceptibly as a whole through new and bold simplicity.

The forms of the sails that constitute the roof of the Opera House, touching a height of 221 feet (about half the height of the nearby Harbour Bridge), closely resemble each other. They face into an ideal direction of the wind, which supports and

from the original design were unable to alter its essence, and his white sails will continue to represent the building and his work as long as the Opera House stands.

The building, whose total construction costs amounted to 102 million Australian dollars, was inaugurated on November 20, 1973 in the presence of Queen Elizabeth II, with the performance of Beethoven's Ninth Symphony. After receiving the Pritzker Prize from the Hyatt Foundation, the Opera House was nominated for UNESCO's World Heritage List.

Numerous proposals have been made for rebuilding its

Sydney Opera House

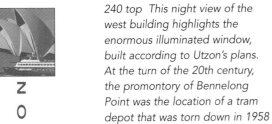

240 top This night view of the west building highlights the enormous illuminated window, built according to Utzon's plans. At the turn of the 20th century, the promontory of Bennelong Point was the location of a tram depot that was torn down in 1958 in order to build the new theater.

240 bottom The interior of the "Guillaume at Bennelong" restaurant offers a stunning view of the city.

241 The curved and uneven outline of the Opera House introduces powerful contrast and spectacular formal innovation to the urban panorama, adding new sightlines and celebrating the city with great expressive capacity.

interiors and the redefining its layout. In 1999 Utzon, his son Jan, and the Australian architect Richard Johnson of Johnson Pilton Walker were commissioned to develop a set of design principles to serve as guidelines for all future changes to the building.

The first proposed change was the construction of a colonnade on the west side of the building, 148 feet long and 16.5 feet wide, inspired by those of the Maya temples. Its aim was to create a spatial and functional relationship between the Studio, Playhouse and Drama Theatre, and allow the foyer to open onto the magnificent view of Sydney Harbour. One of the rooms of the Opera House has been named after the architect, in recognition of his great achievement and as a token of gratitude for having given Sydney a universal symbol. The room is the only authentic Utzon interior in the building and is used for concerts as well as

children's activities. The refurbishing included the installation of a 46-foot-long floor-to-ceiling tapestry designed by the architect himself and inspired by Bach's Brandenburg Concertos and Raphael's "Procession to Calvary"; work on the tapestry was supervised by Utzon's daughter.

The Opera Theatre and Concert Hall have been the subject of detailed acoustic surveys performed in collaboration with musicians and orchestra conductors and with the Australian Chamber Orchestra. Studies have also been conducted on sound diffusion, stage equipment, accessibility and air conditioning, using modern technologies that will permit considerable functional improvement that would have been impossible until only recently. (Francesco Boccia)

242-243 and 242 bottom left This overhead view illustrates the integration of the structures of the Cultural Center with their natural surroundings. The conical huts of the existing village served as a model for the project, which interprets their form and building materials. This view shows the entrance portico that connects the buildings of the Cultural Center and protects visitors from the sun by offering them plenty of shady areas.

242 bottom right The layout drawing illustrates the linear distribution of the Cultural Center and the orientation of Piano's "huts," which face the bay, symbolically welcoming the ocean breeze.

243 The different sizes and heights of the individual buildings sketch out a dynamic and complex contour, eschewing regular and uniform lines, which would be unsuitable for this completely natural setting.

DESIGN	CONSTRUCTION	DIMENSIONS	USE
R. PIANO	1991-1998	TOTAL AREA 861,113 SQUARE FT	CULTURAL CENTER

LAGUNE

LAGON

Centre Culturel Tjibaou

NOUMÉA, NEW CALEDONIA

The encounter of advanced western construction technologies with the indigenous tradition of the Kanak has generated one of the most fascinating and evocative works of architecture of the last century. The cultural center that Renzo Piano designed in New Caledonia was funded entirely by the French government to commemorate Jean-Marie Tjibaou, who was assassinated in 1989. The political upheaval that led to the death of the leader of the independent movement ultimately helped the country gain its independence, which was fully legitimated by François Mitterand and honored with the construction of this village of culture and art.

The first aspect of Piano's project involved interpreting the setting. Drawing on local forms and materials, his plans envisaged ten wood-and-steel huts of different sizes, set amidst columnar pines along the promontory of the island

spaced to allow the ocean winds to blow through them. As the winds penetrate the wooden framework of the huts, they transform them into vibrating sound boxes. Copying the typical form of Maori huts, the technology adopted here employs a range of different materials. Alongside reeds, sand, bark and plant fibers, the architect used laminated wood, coral, glass, concrete, cast aluminum and steel tie rods.

The advantages of modern construction techniques have been combined with the local weather conditions to increase the efficiency of natural ventilation and cooling. The double roofing layer allows the monsoon air blowing in from the sea to circulate in the interspace, naturally cooling the work areas and minimizing the use of mechanical equipment needed to control air conditioning and temperature.

To avoid creating (as Piano himself put it) "something

and outlined against the multicolor sky of Polynesia The arrangement of the buildings facing the shore of the bay of Nouméa encourages nature walks, leading visitors from one point of the complex to another along the "path of history" designed by anthropologist Alban Bensa to illustrate the life and legends of the Pacific communities.

Solidly anchored to the ground, the huts rise in curved shell shapes of different heights. They house exhibition space for shows devoted to the works of local artists, offices, the library, a conference room and school recreation areas where painting, dance and crafts courses are held.

The most unique feature of these dwellings is their structure, composed of iroko slats and staves that are

folkloric and kitschy," the design of the traditional crown-like top of the Maori huts was reinterpreted by lowering the vertical elements to give the shells a more open form. The precise alignment of the ten structures set amidst vegetation evokes the powerful eloquence of the enormous Moai, the stone sculptures on Rapa Nui (Easter Island). This demonstrates that it is not necessarily true that the work of modern man – unlike that of the ancients – is always invasive and uses methods that are harmful for the environment. Piano's integration of technology and nature, future and tradition, has yielded deeply emotional results, reflecting undisputed faith in experimentation and research that move beyond the fads and labels of so many contemporary linguistic approaches. (Matteo Agnoletto)

Centre Culturel Tjibaou

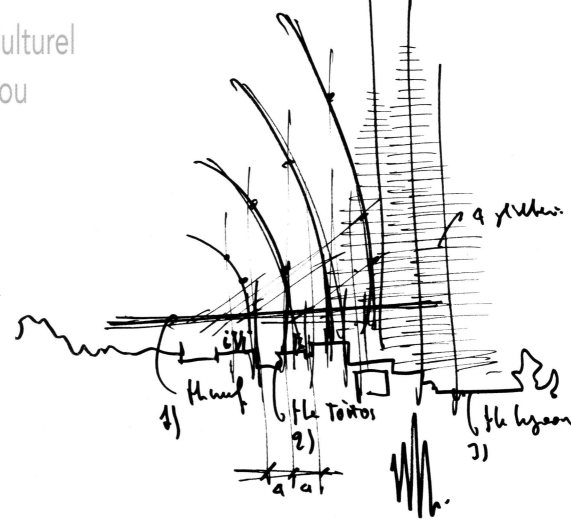

244 and 245 Renzo Piano's study sketch shows the relationship between the curves of the shells and the framework of the façades. The wooden cladding of the "huts" forges a relationship with the vegetation. As can clearly be seen, the construction skeleton used here is made of wood with steel tie rods. The openings left between the wooden staves are covered with grids. The different heights form a lightweight crown that opens up to frame the sky. The new huts are also sonorous architectures: when the ocean breeze blows through the openings in the structure, the staves vibrate, producing an enchanting musical sound.

Centre Culturel Tjibaou

246 and 247 top The rooms inside the Cultural Center house exhibitions devoted to local art and civilization. The project strived for a sense of harmony with the local tradition. At the same time, by adopting advanced and innovative technologies, it also offers the amenities needed by users. The ten "huts" are completely hollow inside, in order to permit maximum use and flexibility in managing the collections.

247 center and bottom The modular system used to finish the interior evokes the open weave of the external facing, concealing the lighting system and air-conditioning equipment, which is supplemented by natural ventilation channeled in through the double roof. As a whole, the Cultural Center is an evocative concept that develops modern architecture by integrating it with the traditions of the native populations of New Caledonia.

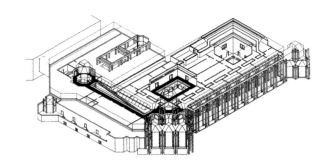

National Gallery of Canada

OTTAWA, CANADA

Situated in one of Ottawa's loveliest settings, the National Gallery overlooks the Ottawa River, facing the Parliament Building and Major's Hill Park. Established in 1980, the institution had changed venues several times over the years.

In 1983 the firm of Moshe Safdie was chosen to design the new complex to house the collection. His museum, which was inaugurated in 1988, boasts the world's largest collection of Canadian art, ranging from religious works to those of the contemporary avant-garde movements, and from painting to sculpture and photography. It thus represents an ideal way to explore the country's artistic culture.

During the early planning phases, two opposite concepts were weighed. The first called for an "introverted" plan, in which the galleries were organized along distribution lines so that the side facing the city was essentially closed.

The winning design overturned these principles, proposing an "extroverted" plan in which a columned portico extends from the entrance to the Great Hall, opening the interior to the city and creating a seamless urban landscape.

The access ramp, lined with columns, gently leads from the entrance pavilion to the Great Hall, a completely transparent structure set opposite the historic Parliament building on the other side of the Ottawa River.

The Great Hall is also where the institution's main public events are held. The structure, which combines concrete, steel and glass, boasts an enormous dome that is the hallmark of this building, which is set on the rocky promontory of Nepean Point, and serves as a visual and cultural benchmark. At the same time, the dome also helps regulate the ambient conditions inside an essentially transparent construction located in the coldest capital city in the world.

Inside the dome, which is 470 feet tall, fabric panels, regulated by remote control, adjust the amount of lighting based on the angle of sunlight.

In its internal layout, the National Gallery resembles the organization of a city. In fact, streets, squares and gardens – some outdoors, other protected by glazed partitions – and various kinds of buildings can be discerned. This forms a

DESIGN	CONSTRUCTION	DIMENSIONS	USE
M. SAFDIE	1986-1988	TOTAL AREA 599,550 SQUARE FT	MUSEUM, ARCHIVES, OFFICES, AREAS FOR EDUCATIONAL PROGRAMS

248 top The isometric projection of the upper gallery emphasizes the path of the ramp that connects the two overlaid levels.

248 center Because of its position on the promontory of Nepean Point, the National Gallery is the focal point of the sprawling public spaces along the Ottawa River, which separates Ontario from Quebec. The museum is across from the solid volume of the Parliament Building.

248 bottom The south side faces Major's Hill Park, an enormous open space that connects the public offices along Sussex Drive with the area along Wellington Street and Rideau Street.

249 The Great Hall, which is reflected in the Ottawa River and projects the city towards the river and Parliament Hill, is surrounded by the green area that starts at Major's Hill Park and extends along Nepean Point and the riverbank.

National Gallery of Canada

250 and 251 top The vertical supports are arranged around "lanterns" that are connected at the top of the dome. The triangular fabric panels can be adjusted to regulate the amount of light in the Great Hall.

251 bottom left The access ramp ascends from the entrance pavilion to the Great Hall, and the path is punctuated by columns and the bearing structures of the skylight.

251 bottom right The indoor garden on the lower level forms a meditative space that faces the galleries, which display Canadian artwork, and it offers visitors a delightful break before they continue their tour.

microcosm in which various functions are juxtaposed and overlap, following a layout in which public spaces rotate around the exhibition areas. The galleries are located on two floors and, connected to the "streets," they sketch out three differentiated courts. Rooms with works by Canadian artists are set along the path ascending from the entrance pavilion to the Great Hall, and they overlook the Water Court and the Garden Court.

Proceeding from the glazed Great Hall to the administrative wing, visitors come to the areas exhibiting contemporary art, which form the Contemporary Court.

Through the combination of glass walls, skylights and slender columns, both of the gallery floors are flooded with natural light. The architecture thus becomes a luminous ambience in which the boundaries between interior and exterior vanish. Diffused light entering from all sides creates an entrancing atmosphere, beckoning visitors to stroll along paths and through gardens – but without ever exiting the structure.

With the National Gallery, Safdie successfully merged nature with architecture, erecting a building that has become an integral part of its surroundings. Through its visual counterpart of Parliament Hill, it acts as a bridge between the present and the cultural heritage of the past. (Guya Elisabetta Rosso)

252 The dome of the Great Hall is a distinctive landmark on the Ottawa skyline.

252-253 On the lower level, the contemporary art gallery combines artificial lighting with natural light, which is let in through a skylight illuminated by the upper floor of the building.

253 top Located on the floor above Rideau Chapel, the gallery dedicated to European and American art is a rectangular space with skylights to let in natural light.

253 bottom The layout of the galleries forms different spaces in order to exploit the sunshine that comes through the skylights. On the lower lever, the barrel vault in the gallery showcasing the works of Canadian artists is crossed by a long shaft of light.

National Gallery
of Canada

Seattle Public Library

SEATTLE, USA

The Central Library in Seattle, Washington, achieves extraordinary sculptural tension. Designed by the Dutch architect Rem Koolhaas of the OMA firm, it redefines the rapport between reading areas and spaces devoted to multimedia activities, lending new meaning to technological forms of expression and information, perceived as equivalent and complementary to traditional printed media.

The building, completed in May 2004, cost over 110 million dollars. The library covers a total area of 412,000 square feet, which includes not only the internal space but also 50,000 square feet of parking.

The building, whose form the architect has compared to a fortress, is profoundly influenced by new high-tech means of communication. It thus becomes an emporium of information, a space for users of all ages. It is open for reading but is also a place designed to explore knowledge. Thus, it is far removed from the simple classification of type, which is recovered and reinterpreted according to concepts that are functional yet free.

The new library – an unmistakable landmark – is outlined against the Washington sky. It is compressed within a compact but complex volume that is divided into three horizontal bands distinguished by iconographic references to geometric primitives. They are enclosed by a uniform yet fragmented façade that replicates the slope between 4th Avenue and Madison Street, multiplying and deconstructing it in a kaleidoscope of images that mirror the surrounding city, likewise fragmented and distorted. This complex of faceted images is augmented by the surface texture of the building's skin, divided into steel-and-glass lozenges that give the existing city yet another grid and suck light into the library's cavernous rooms. The outcome is a natural interplay of light and shadows that is not actively exploited, but knowingly and joyously embraced.

The library distributes the information destined for its users, organizing it on eight floors whose horizontal levels are alternated with the free movement of the skin of the structure. This physical accumulation follows a linear path that generates a sense of motion, in spaces that are perceived as urban and are flexible enough to accommodate the spontaneous development of activities. This avoids arbitrary descriptions and delimitations, while maintaining notable attributes in terms of numbers. In fact, when the library was inaugurated, it held 780,000 books on 6233 shelves, but it can be expanded to hold 1,450,000 books without requiring any additional modules.

This masterly organization of space and flow, conceived according to criteria of analogy, creates interaction among the various subject areas. For example, the sequence of book collections is defined on the floor by progressive numeric codes.

The decrease in natural light as one moves towards the interior is offset by the architect's bold and impeccable color scheme. The walls of the reading rooms are purple, the escalators and stairwells are yellow, and the meeting areas are red.

At night, the reflected portrait of the city offers a glimpse of the library's intriguing and distinctive interior. This does not alter the vision of the complex as a whole, but simply portrays it from a different vantage point, with platforms that seem to float in the darkness of Seattle. The library earned Koolhaas the Honor Award for Architecture from the American Institute of Architects. (Francesco Boccia)

DESIGN	CONSTRUCTION	DIMENSIONS	USE
R. KOOLHAAS	2001-2004	TOTAL AREA 412,258 SQUARE FT	LIBRARY, ANNEXED PARKING

254 This view of the Seattle Public Library creates a dazzling contrast between the internal partitions and the structural elements: the floors seem to float against the sky, revealing their internal spaces and spatial complexity.

254-255 and 255 bottom The volumes composing the building follow the slope of the street and incorporate it in the design, multiplying it and drawing it into the connections between the main sections.

R. KOOLHAAS

Seattle Public Library

256 and 256-257 Inside the reading room and the Living Room on the third floor, the light from outside casts the shadows of the lozenge-shaped windowpanes onto the floor, decorated with Petra Blaisse's floral motifs. The concept of space devoted to meditation is linked with a clear perception of the passage of time.

257 top The steel-and-glass cladding of the building affords a view of the surrounding urban space, but it is also an element of formal continuity within the library. All the areas open to library users thus benefit from natural lighting throughout the day.

257 bottom The connective space distributes the routes crossing the various areas of the library. Glass walls – which allow natural light into the enormous spaces, protected by the clear roofing formed by diamond-shaped panels – make it possible to observe the area set aside for users as well as the one reserved for the administrative offices and open only to employees.

258 Koolhaas used contrasting colors to make the compositional and functional elements of the building immediately recognizable, with bold color schemes that reflect extraordinary design clarity. The escalators linking the floors are an example: the railings, side walls and ceilings have been painted phosphorescent yellow.

259 top One of the conference rooms on the fourth floor is designed as an organic maze. Every element connecting the various rooms is marked by the same shade of red.

259 center The books are set along a spiral path: signs on the staircases of each of the four floors indicate the literary genre of that floor.

259 bottom left and center The reading room has simple square pillars and the ceiling is lined with special material to absorb sound.

259 bottom right The Mixing Chamber is an area the architect designed to encourage interaction among library habitués.

Seattle Public Library

260 The entrance to the fourth level of the library and the connection corridors abandon straight lines and soft colors. Bright red stairs, designed with curved lines and rounded corners, lead to the heart of the building and the conference rooms.

261 The routes to the fire escapes, whose vertical and horizontal surfaces are all painted the same color, create a sense of disorientation, as the boundaries between the floors, walls and ceiling are barely perceptible. These transit areas are also red.

Seattle Public Library

262 top The San Francisco Museum of Modern Art stands out as a solid and steady presence in this West Coast city, where urban transformation has adapted to a constantly changing society.

262 bottom The purpose of the 45-degree slope is to bring as much light as possible into the interior. The enormous cylindrical skylight was created by combining a metal framework and structural skeleton with precast elements finished with brickwork.

San Francisco Museum of Modern Art

SAN FRANCISCO, USA

Overlooking the Yerba Buena Gardens and located near the Visual Art Center surrounded by three buildings on an American scale, the Museum of Modern Art is a solid presence in the bustling residential district known as SoMa, or South of Market.

The setting is powerfully marked by architectural works, as the park boasts Fumihiko Maki's Centre for the Arts Gallery and James Polshek's Centre for the Arts Theater.

Inaugurated in 1995 for the museum's 60th anniversary, the new building is the second largest of its kind devoted to modern art in the United States.

According to the goals set by the museum and shared by the architect, natural lighting, a recognizable image, and the uniformity of the interior represent the founding principles of the plans.

Despite the ratio between lot size and constructed surface, diffuse light – difficult to achieve in a project in

cladding. The patterned brickwork is set at different angles to give these surfaces intriguing dynamism, refracting sunlight into stark chiaroscuro.

The contrast with setting is provocative, triggering a dialectical comparison between construction philosophies. The stacked monolithic volumes rise in a stepped layout to reveal the cylindrical central tower, which is distinguished by the two-tone interplay of marble bands radiating around the skylight, which is tilted at a 45° angle.

Along the side, the juxtaposition of the fire escape acquires significance through the use of brickwork. It duplicates the inclination of the stepped façade, following the changes in slope and emphasizing them with pale stone inserts.

DESIGN	CONSTRUCTION	DIMENSIONS	USE
M. BOTTA	1992-1995	USABLE AREA 199,132 SQUARE FT	MUSEUM, OFFICES, MULTIPURPOSE AREAS

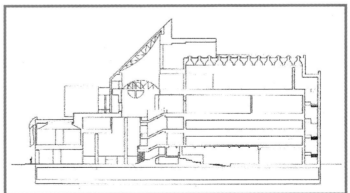

which the solidity of the façades predominates over openings – is let in mainly from skylights, making it possible to illuminate the exhibited works evenly.

For the façades, the decision to propose a surface with a uniform yet textured character led to the idea of juxtaposing the concrete-and-steel structure with brick

The back of the museum is composed of five towers that house the administrative offices and the galleries. A low colonnade – and, here too, horizontal black-and-white bands have been used for the columns – lead into the enormous space of the central atrium. This internal plaza distributes the interior both horizontally and vertically, up

262-263 The siting of the museum, surrounded by very tall buildings, generated a highly unconventional structure that eschews any stylistic comparison with its surroundings. Three guidelines were followed in designing the museum: the creation of an exterior surface that would not reveal the face of the structure, enticing the visitor to seek the countenance within; the creation of a cogent internal image; and the exploitation of natural lighting for the interior.

San Francisco Museum of Modern Art

to the summit that lets in natural light.

The interior is laid out on cantilevered floors, which narrow towards the top of the building and are awash in zenithal light.

In order to link the different parts of the museum and create a recognizable path, only a limited array of materials has been used, creating a contrast between the chalky white walls and the gleaming black granite flooring.

Set around the atrium are the bookshop, the café and the auditorium, which extends towards the back of the building perpendicular to Third Street.

From the second to the fourth floor, the exhibition spaces

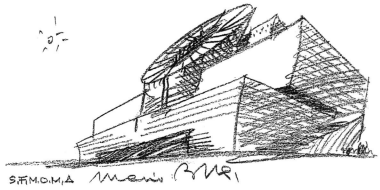

are set around the central atrium. On the fifth floor, a metal catwalk crosses the cylindrical body and leads to the room housing temporary exhibitions.

In addition to museum activities and a library with a collection of about 85,000 books, the SFMoMA also offers numerous public spaces for meetings and conventions, as well as multimedia areas for exhibition-related events. (Guya Elisabetta Rosso)

264 With its sloped lateral face, the museum serves as a link between the horizontal extension of the park and the vertical lines of the buildings behind it. The cylindrical tower emerges from the square blocks and breaks up their symmetry, creating profound shadows that frame the block, emphasized by the two-tone bands radiating from the round skylight.

264-265 The construction of the museum complex as a point of arrival of the itinerary that includes the park and the Visual Art Center makes SFMOMA a new cultural reference point for the city.

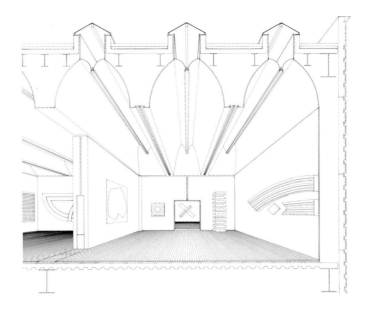

San Francisco Museum of Modern Art

266 top and bottom left The cross section shows how natural light is brought into the exhibition rooms, illuminating them from overhead. Diffuse lighting pervades the space and the exhibited works. Natural lighting was one of the principles inspiring the design of the museum.

266 bottom right At the base of the cylindrical tower, three chalky white columns rise from the black granite floor that juxtaposes polished and rough bands. The distinction between light and dark, glossy and opaque, is reflected in the contrast between diffuse lighting and the shaft of light streaming in from overhead.

267 The staircases that follow the circular movement of the cylindrical section lead visitors to the gallery on the top floor. A walkway suspended over the central space, dominated by the enormous skylight, connects the circulation and exhibitions areas.

Walt Disney Concert Hall

LOS ANGELES, USA

Located at the intersection of 1st Street and Grand Avenue on Bunker Hill, the Walt Disney Concert Hall represents the cultural and architectural revival of downtown Los Angeles.

The project to build the concert hall named after the father of American cartoons began when Lillian Disney, Walt Disney's widow, donated 50 million dollars to the Los Angeles Philharmonic. This opened a brand-new chapter in the history of West Coast architecture and in the city's search for a

DESIGN	CONSTRUCTION	DIMENSIONS	USE
F. GEHRY	1999-2003	TYPICAL FLOOR AREA: 200,209 SQUARE FT	AUDITORIUM, REHEARSAL ROOM, SHOPS, RESTAURANT, UNDERGROUND PARKING

distinctive identity. The plans submitted to the competition had to address three main design tenets. The top priority was to create a venue that would involve the audience by creating a rapport with the musicians through perfect acoustics. Secondly, the building had to serve as the mirror and symbol of Los Angeles' multifaceted culture and climate, offering residents a welcoming and hospitable public place.

Lastly, the new construction had to create a link with the existing Music Center and Museum of Contemporary Art, while also helping to revitalize the Bunker Hill area.

In addition to the technical requirements established by the panel responsible for awarding the commission, Lillian Disney had her own request: passionate about gardens, she wanted one included in the project.

The original competition plans underwent numerous changes. An initial version called for a building constructed entirely of limestone, but metal panels were used instead to help keep costs down and guarantee a more earthquake-proof structure. Stone was thus used only for the office block and the backstage building at the corner of Second and Hope Streets.

The enormous urban sculpture of the Walt Disney Music Hall rises on the lot delimited by First and Second Streets, Grand Avenue, and Hope Street. The building is rotated towards the Museum of Contemporary Art (MoCA), giving LA a "metropolitan rendezvous" at the intersection of Grand Avenue and First Street, in the form of the glass foyer with a garden. This space also serves as a sprawling open civic area and gathering place for residents flocking to the Music Hall, MoCA and the Music Center.

The two floors of the Concert Hall are the focal point for the service space. The main hall is the heart of the building. Gehry's starting point was his desire to mold a space that would be unique not only in terms of acoustics, but that would also create an intimate atmosphere. In order to address acoustical needs, he turned to the consulting firm of Nagata Acoustics, seeking to combine visual and aural perception so that the architectural environment would have a decisive influence on the perception of sound.

From the outside, the hall looks like a ship, but inside the interplay of recesses and billowing structures divides the space into five different levels. All the spatial lines extend from the

268 In 1988 the firm, which was still quite small, was forced to revolutionize its design approach, turning to a method based on software used in the aerospace industry. The production of digital working drawings made it possible to monitor the entire project from concept to completion, introducing a fully computerized process to the field of construction for the very first time.

268-269 and 269 bottom The appearance of the building plays on the geological nature of the city, which is all too familiar with the effects of earthquakes. Thus, it evokes the local geology through centrifugal motion that expands from the main hall towards the outside and involves all its volumes in a virtual tremblor that twists and expands it, creating a contrast with the inflexible grid of downtown Los Angeles.

platform of the orchestra conductor, who metaphorically directs the entire building.

In order to fit the interior space into the shell, other utilities have been set in the interstices, offering different viewpoints and ways of using this space.

The impact of the Walt Disney Concert Hall on public opinion cannot be considered moderate by any means. The controversy surrounding it spared neither promoters nor citizens, with the building being accused of a multitude of sins, from seeking to quench the city's thirst for eccentric architecture and not matching the Disney image, to consisting of a shapeless heap of garbage.
(Guya Elisabetta Rosso)

270 top The shell is composed of three layers: wood and plaster were used for the interior, the middle layer holds the steel framework, and steel panels form the skin.

270 center In the main auditorium, which can hold up to 2265 people, every seat enjoys an excellent view and extraordinary acoustics.

270 bottom and 271 Though the double-height space created areas of sharp contrast between light and shadow, the different materials that have been used merge in an interpenetration of forms, which open up unexpectedly to reveal skylights that illuminate these composite spaces.

272-273 The stainless-steel panels reflect the California sunshine.

Walt Disney Concert Hall

274-275 The view of the south façade demonstrates how Eisenmen has taken up – and deconstructed – the image of the tower of the old armory, a fortress-like structure that was destroyed by fire. Like most of the building, the tower rooms are below ground level.

274 bottom In his plans for the Wexner Center for the Arts, architect Peter Eisenman designed an exhibition space that would respond to the needs of 21st-century art. The bodies of the building are set in the free areas between the extant structures.

DESIGN	CONSTRUCTION	DIMENSIONS	USE
P. Eisenman	1983-1989	Total area 581,251 square ft	Museum, events room, library, film center, cafeteria, exhibition space

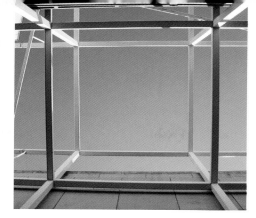

275 top *The picture shows a detail of the three-dimensional white grid that, like a backbone for the entire construction, extends around the two older buildings. The grid marks the route between the different buildings of the Wexner Center.*

275 bottom *The plan concept underscores the conflict between the specificity of place and a deformed vision of that space. This vision is pursued by attempting to deprive the physical center of its role as the functional core of a building, which must offer itself as a space intended for a particular yet indeterminate function.*

Wexner Center for the Arts

COLUMBUS, USA

Born in New Jersey in 1932, Peter Eisenman is one of the leading representatives of deconstructionism. The American architect designed the Wexner Center for the Arts in Columbus, Ohio (United States), completed in 1989, for which he received the 1993 National Honor Award from the American Institute of Architects. Culturally influenced by the works of Andrea Palladio and Giuseppe Terragni, Eisenman gained worldwide acclaim through an extensive series of prestigious projects and works.

The Columbus museum is an intriguing design experience, created with the intent of generating a new relationship between exhibited art and museum architecture.

Eisenman's plans responded specifically to the competition requirements, which called for a museum space designed to house 21st-century art.

The new museum was to be situated on the campus of Ohio State University. The concept proposed by Eisenman breaks up and warps the university's orthogonal layout, which is offset by about 12.5° with respect to the urban grid and thus created a rift between city and campus. Consequently, the museum reestablishes the three-dimensional lines of the city grid. Eisenman decided not to occupy one of the free areas of the campus with a new building, instead conceiving

276 and 277 In designing the dense structural framework of the Wexner Center for the Arts, Eisenman – whose early studies were influenced by the works of the Italian architect Giuseppe Terragni – proposed a succession of vertical elements, whose form takes up the lines of the painted metal structure on the outside. This external structure, which resembles scaffolding, symbolizes an unfinished work ever in progress. The three-dimensional rhythm of the grid is evoked inside by the windowpanes and the ceiling patterns.

Wexner Center for the Arts

the volumes of his museum in the open areas between the existing buildings.

The different parts of the architectural complex are connected by enormous painted metal scaffolding, symbolizing a work ever in progress. Its modular rhythm is repeated in the interior, in the form of false ceilings and windowed sections. Inside, a gallery-route that is used as a transit area connects the lobby and the auditorium to the library, projection rooms, cinema, art rooms, a video postproduction studio, a bookshop, a café and 12,000 square feet of gallery space.

The southeast corner takes up the image of the old armory, a fortress-like structure that was destroyed in a fire in 1958, and thus effectively evokes the history of the site. However, the construction is fragmented, suggesting that the past cannot truly be recovered and perceived, but only recounted with narrative and formal discontinuity. The offices inside the tower have windows on the roof level, as most of the building is underground.

The main staircase features the famous suspended pillar, the bottom of which is visible about ten feet above the visitors' heads. The idea of potential new art forms – laser beams, videos, live performances, moving expressions – convinced Eisenman to reject the rigid continuity typical of other museums, composed of a sequence of rooms. Thus, his concept makes the artists responsible for defining, delimiting and completing the space with their works: they appropriate the performance space, light and time, and – ultimately – the visitor's attention. At the same time, by Eisenman's own definition this concept brings the museum close to "shopping centers next to highways" and imposes critical, raucous spatiality composed of enormous rows of pillars: the dramatic vision of deconstructed space.

The Wexner Center opened in November 1989 and was named after Leslie Wexner, the founder of Limited Brands and the philanthropist who funded the museum. Though it mainly houses temporary exhibits, it also has a permanent work by Maya Lin, designed for the exterior of the building. (Francesco Boccia)

278 top The interlocking of
the internal concrete structure
and the external glazing
makes Ambasz's oeuvre
unique. His works show a
recurrent motif: he buries
functional systems, only to
make a sign of their presence
emerge.

278 top The interlocking of
the internal concrete structure
and the external glazing
makes Ambasz's oeuvre
unique. His works show a
recurrent motif: he buries
functional systems, only to
make a sign of their presence
emerge.

278 bottom The plans for the
Halsell Conservatory addressed
the need to create a botanical
garden in the hot dry climate of
Texas. The tallest plants grow in
the glazed part of the
greenhouses, whereas the buried
portion, which remains cool, is
almost invisible from the outside.

Lucille Halsell Conservatory
SAN ANTONIO, USA

Emilio Ambasz: the quintessential narrator. He is the bard of a world he wants to portray as self-balanced and, indeed, wants to rebalance in its overall relationship with the elements comprising it.

His is a world of sweeping spaces, greenery, trees, and water, and a culture that is minimalist in its own way, that steps in just enough with an attitude held by few in the realm of design, as most of its representatives are often – if not always – intent on or trained to interpret architecture solely as built works. The areas of intervention are indifferent – if not hostile – to the lifestyle of their occupants. In historic districts and sprawling suburbs alike, they are crushed by sheer artificiality: in climate, in the orientation of buildings, and in overall livability entrusted to bureaucratic statistics and percentages that codify heights and footage, materials and insulation. In short, artificial. All in all, Ambasz is the man who demolished contextual terms, reordering them as much

as possible, and in every condition or situation. He has organized his work based on a philosophy that speaks the language of a possible utopia. Here, the overall system of the sense of space, of its reflexes and influence over increasingly urbanized humanity, has been projected based on a philosophy that, as in the works of Frank Lloyd Wright, is linked with immense spaces – in this case, perhaps the memory of the boundless vistas of Argentina.

But when necessary he intervenes in shards of urban territory – as frequently occurs in Japan and elsewhere – with works that are full-fledged manifestos of the possibility of reproposing applications and alternative paths that have been created using what technology has to offer. This possible utopia is progressive.

In this case, the revival or affirmation of the use of greenery as the main design tool reigns supreme and has nothing to do with camouflage or furnishings. Ambasz has few precedents in this. Generally, in the history of architecture there has been a form of

DESIGN	CONSTRUCTION	DIMENSIONS	USE
E. AMBASZ	1982	TOTAL AREA 90,094 SQUARE FT	BOTANICAL GARDEN

279 Interrupted forms and
obelisks – old and alive,
like the plant life in the
greenhouses – fit in perfectly

with any type of external
nature, which never
dominates but instead
magnifies them.

Lucille Halsell Conservatory

mediation between nature and artifice, *natura naturans* and *natura naturata*, in which the latter – with the exception of the Hanging Gardens of Babylon – is accessory to the former and not its primary element, regardless of any orographic difficulties.

The Pompeian villa interpenetrated the vegetation of its courtyards. The superfluous and the necessary were integrated, only to become separated starting with the Renaissance, when the garden became "the other manmade work" and an element to be experienced by admiring it. This followed a condition that rationalism itself had emphasized, striking a balance between the world of artificiality and nature that was biased towards the former.

Ville Savoye interprets the "superior" equidistance of the manmade and the perfection of reason as the stage for the contraposition that is necessary and probably inevitable between the two natures. Barragan, the great Mexican architect, brought reason itself to a different confrontation with its surroundings. His partitions, his colored slabs and water set out to emphasize the

a single well around which the non-manmade was organized. With Ambasz, this concept is marked by what rises from the ground or by the presence of a manmade work that is rarely solid. In some cases, the work itself is hard to discern from the floor levels, where it is impossible to visualize the modicum of symbolic anthropomorphism that is usually present in plan views: it is far easier to glean from a bird's-eye view. We are referring to circumferences, the geometry of primitive forms, and the irregularity of nature organized almost in a form of self-design.

This is what happens with the plans for the greenhouses of the Lucille Halsell Conservatory in San Antonio, Texas. Here, the climate itself has encouraged certain aspects, such as the partial and even total burial of several crops that would otherwise be subject to the external environmental aridity. Thus, the most suitable microclimate has been created.

The result is the surprising invention of an urban layout with an indefinable chronological dimension, transparent and imbued with

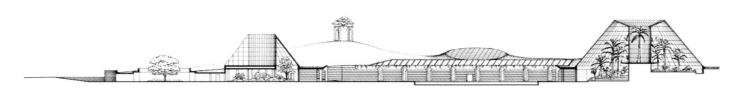

power of the landscape as the indispensable presence of design, of which they are neither a metaphor nor an integration. And there is no doubt that Barragan is ideally close to the philosophy of Ambasz. What they have in common are sweeping spaces and the non-negation of the symbolic value of architecture (moving away from Wright, in this case), as well as the non-imperative but ever-present affirmation of historic origins and erudite allusions, along the lines of Mies van der Rohe in the case of Barragan, the singular organic rationalist of the new world.

Ambasz is more flexible. He loves territorial and orographic discontinuity, and exploits it to bury himself in it, akin to what once occurred at several presaharian settlements, where light came from

formal and psychological suggestions. By burying functions, Ambasz brings to the surface truncated pyramids and cones whose sole purpose seems to be that of offering themselves to the landscape, virtually the relics of a technologically advanced society like the high level of finish of the greenhouses, because this is their function.

The remains of ponds, light, and absolute forms – albeit manipulated – create this incredible archaeology of the present that distances itself from any classical reference that may be familiar to us. Like enormous radars or the astronomical observatories of Agra, they turn to an absolute that is ineffable and incomprehensible, but one with an extraordinary impact. (Silvio Cassarà)

280 and 280-281 The frustum area of the greenhouses with the palm trees exploits the partially buried area and creates staggered levels that are intriguing from a spatial and functional standpoint. The circles of the layout become cones in elevation, and the squares morph into pyramids, giving these forms ancient, ancestral auras and meanings.

281 bottom The roofs of the greenhouses of the Lucille Halsell Conservatory interpret the panorama of the future through the forms of the past – or perhaps of timelessness itself. This involves sophisticated construction technology, with spaces that seem to exclude the human presence that created them and through the knowledge that is presented in a seemingly disorderly and random assemblage of forms.

Guggenheim Museum

NEW YORK, USA

The Guggenheim Museum in New York is one of Frank Lloyd Wright's most famous works and marks a watershed in museum architecture, moving beyond the usual concept of this type of space as a sequence of rooms with no relation to each other or the outside.

Hilla Rebay, curator of the collection, originally asked Wright to design the museum, which was to house Solomon R. Guggenheim's collection of abstract paintings, in the summer of

continuum. The eye does not encounter the intersection of contrasting surfaces but is gently drawn into an "unbreaking wave" that binds vertical tension – leading up to the luminous cupola – with the horizontality of organic architecture.

The internal space moves along several levels, enveloping yet also liberating the visitor, allowing him to create his own personal itinerary. The visit is thus transformed into an experience, in which space – and the works exhibited in that space – can be perceived differently on every level.

1943. He was asked to create an architectural setting that would reflect the revolutionary character of the works it would contain.

Well before the work commenced, the architect's plans sparked an enormous outcry. It was thought that such an evocative setting would distract people, detracting from the works displayed in it. The architect later commented that his goal in designing the museum was not to overpower the paintings. "On the contrary, it was to make the building and the painting an uninterrupted, beautiful symphony such as never existed in the world of art before."

The entire building was made of cast concrete, in which the observer does not perceive the superposition of layers but a

From a construction standpoint, one of the most important elements here is light. The natural light that streams in from the central dome and from the continuous band of skylights, which follow the ascending line of the curved walls and are regulated by adjustable translucent shutters, is supplemented by an artificial incandescent lighting system. This creates a subtle connection between the various light sources to ensure their uniformity.

The natural and artificial lighting systems are integrated with form, coalescing with and complementing the exhibited works to create a single ambience, merging container and content.

The sloped internal walls display the works as if they were still sitting on the artist's easel.

282 At first Wright did not agree with the choice of New York as the location for the museum. He felt that the city *was chaotic and overpopulated: a metropolis that often clashes with the concept of nature.*

DESIGN	CONSTRUCTION	DIMENSIONS	USE
F. Lloyd Wright	1956-1959	Total area approximately 46,791 square ft	Museum, library, café, theater, offices

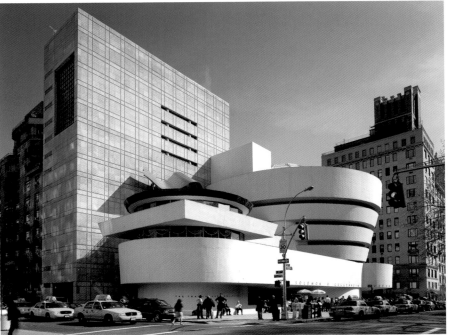

282-283 Though the land was purchased only after the architect had been commissioned for the project, the fact that the museum would be built in an urban setting convinced Wright to establish a relationship between his architecture and Manhattan's vertical thrust, and this is evident even in his earliest sketches.

283 bottom Without relinquishing the horizontality typical of his works, Wright designed a building inspired by the concept of nature and the organic fusion of form and function.

284 and 285 top The choice of pure white for the entire building accentuates the image of an eggshell, a form with enormous sculptural quality that suggests a welcoming ambience. Light shines through window slits to illumine the soft, velvety surface.

285 bottom The works of art are bound to this shell, as they are enveloped yet also liberated by a space designed to show them at their best.

286-287 Inside, all functions are caught up in ascending rotational movement.

Guggenheim Museum

At the Guggenheim Museum, the element of the spiral is brought inside – as opposed to the Gordon Strong Planetarium, for example – to invert interior and exterior, creating a relationship between city and museum. It thus transforms them into an "art walk" that strives to extend the city itself to become reunited with the setting. The visitor's involvement begins before he or she even sets foot in the building: the flowerboxes at the entrance beckon passersby to stop for a moment, and the curvilinear overhang of the connection between the two volumes forms a portico leading to the atrium. Here, the oval fountain marks the starting point of the spiral forming the gallery. Nevertheless, the Guggenheim is also a provocative city-planning work that breaks with tradition, and it was designed to offset the uniform grid of the streets of New York. In this, it served as the springboard for academic and reactionary movements of innovative trends in the Midwest and West. Wright eloquently expressed the concept of a skyscraper as an individual landmark, but without denying the natural environment. The figurative and plastic form of the museum strives to reestablish a link between city and nature. Located on Fifth Avenue at the edge of Central Park, it cogently merges the two through spatial continuity. (Guya Elisabetta Rosso)

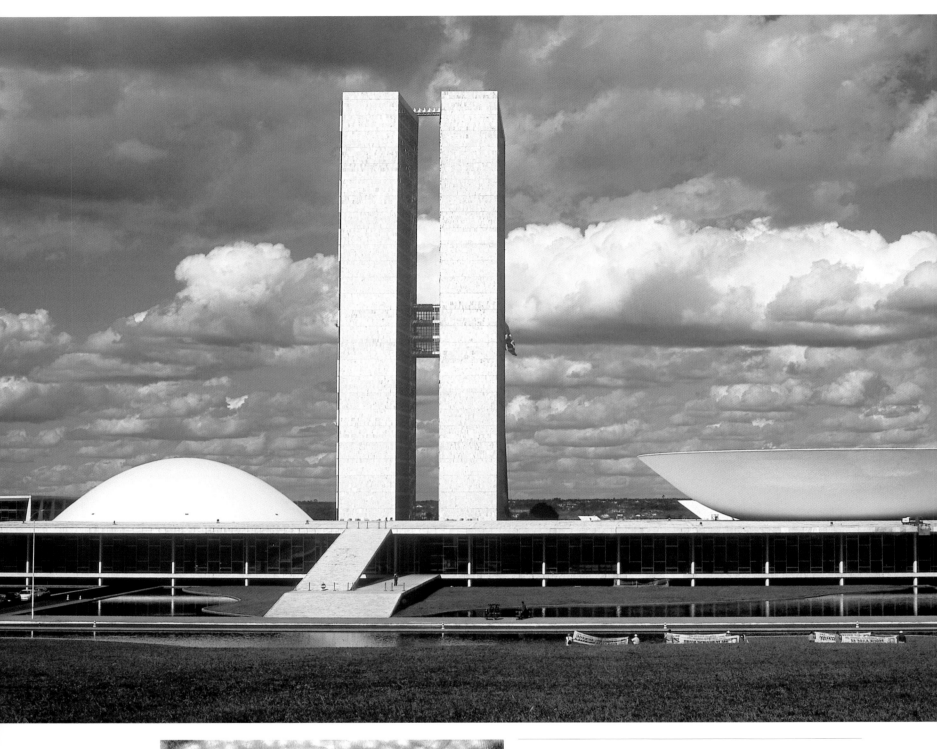

289 The Senate Chamber is an overturned dome, symbolizing the need for the various institutions of government to complement each other.

DESIGN	CONSTRUCTION	DIMENSIONS	USE
O. Niemeyer	1956-1970	Total area 419791 square ft	Institutional buildings, administrative offices

288-289 The ramp that leads to the roof of the Parliament Building, with the towers rising behind it, beckons visitors to move amidst the metaphysical geometric forms of the domes overlooking the Chamber of Deputies and the Senate.

288 bottom left The interior of the Senate Chamber is encircled by a balcony, from which people can observe the sessions.

288 bottom right The Parliament Building is visible in the middle of this aerial view.

The Square of the Three Powers
BRASÍLIA, BRAZIL

I n 1956 Juscelino Kubitschek, Brazil's progressive president, announced a competition to plan the country's new capital city, which was to be built on an uninhabited plateau in the middle of the country. The new city, named Brasília, was to symbolize the desire for social and cultural advancement of this enormous South American nation.

collaboration with Costa; Le Corbusier served as a consultant on the project. Niemeyer subsequently drew up the plans for Pampulha, a suburb of Belo Horizonte, exploring the expressive potential of reinforced concrete and openly criticizing the rationalist creed of right angles.

The heart of the plans for Brasília is the famous Square of

The winning design, submitted by Lúcio Costa, reflected the era's avant-garde city-planning theories, faithfully following the dictates of the famous Athens Charter drawn up by CIAM (Congres Internationaux d'Architecture Moderne) in 1933, in the wake of Le Corbusier's concepts.

Costa conceived of the future capital based on a profoundly symbolic cruciform layout, with a division of space that reflected single-function zoning – a concept that is now obsolete as it ultimately proved to be inhospitable. Nevertheless, it would be inappropriate to write off as a mistake the greatest attempt ever made to create – *in vitro* – a city designed as the expression of progress and democracy. Indeed, the concept of democracy is essential in interpreting the work of Oscar Niemeyer, the architect commissioned by Kubitschek in 1958 to design the buildings for Brasília.

Niemeyer had gained international acclaim in the late Thirties with his plans for the headquarters of the Ministry of Education and Public Health in Rio de Janeiro, in

the Three Powers, which is the focal point of the city. The square symbolizes the balance of legislative, executive and judiciary powers – the soul of democracy – by conceptually positioning the buildings, which represent the various institutional functions, in a triangle.

Niemeyer also decided that each building should symbolize the institutions' proximity to citizens, integrating public paths with the very structure of the buildings, and thus creating a strong and enduring bond. Hence he designed immense porticoes to protect these glass prisms from the broiling sun and torrential rains, and a colossal ramp that leads pedestrians to the roof of the Parliament building. Likewise, broad spaces and the use of glass reflect the architect's desire to make the places of power visually open, contrasting the suppression typical of reactionary ideologies.

Niemeyer's language rejects the stylistic elements of the past in favor of a modern idiom that pursues innovative forms and effective functional solutions, as testified by his careful

The Square of the Three Powers

study of the routes inside the individual buildings. At Brasília he provides yet another example of his ability to interact with the engineers commissioned to design the bearing structures of the individual buildings. These skeletons of reinforced concrete look as if they are about to float away and are anchored to the ground solely by slender tapered supports, with an effect that seems to strike a balance between the scenes of a metaphysical painting and zoomorphism. Indeed, much of Brasília's allure lies in its multifaceted interpretations: viewed from the air, the city can be compared to an airplane or a bird with that has spread its wings, ever poised between nature and artifice, and between dreams and reality.

Despite the fact that it has revealed all the limitations of zoning concepts and that it cost the country a staggering amount of money, the city has been added to UNESCO's World Heritage List, and visiting it is a thought-provoking experience Dotted with small and large masterpieces that evoke the words of the man who, alongside Kubitschek and Costa, masterminded their setting . "[Architecture] is not the most important thing there is. Life is the most important thing – people getting along with each other…. We have to change the world." (Marco Tagliatori)

290 top The elegant interiors are replete with symbolic and stylized references to the free forms of Brazil's natural environment – captivating yet harsh – in the heart of which the capital city of Brasília was built.

290 center, bottom and 209-291 The Parliament Building, the Brazilian Supreme Court Building and the Palácio do Planalto, or the seat of the executive branch, form a triangle symbolizing the division of the three powers (legislative, executive and judiciary) that are the foundations of democracy. In the minds of its promoters, first and foremost President Juscelino Kubitschek, Brasília had to express these ideas. What is evident here is the architect's goal of uniting an image of modernity, through the daring use of reinforced-concrete elements, with a sense of transparency, achieved with enormous glass walls. Statues by renowned artists commissioned to commemorate famous figures in the history of Brazil dot the public space.

The Square of the Three Powers

292-293 and 292 bottom left
The Pantheon was built
behind the Congress Building
in a space dedicated to Lúcio
Costa, the mind behind
Brasília's urban planning. The
delicately balanced Pantheon
evokes a dove poised in
flight.

292 bottom right The dove, the
symbol of peace, is one of
Niemeyer's favorite themes, and he
decided to design a tower to
house these birds in the Square of
the Three Powers. This tower is
also a sculpture that is perfectly
incorporated in the metaphysical
panorama of the Brasília Memorial.

293 Brasília's allure seems be
heightened at night, when the
play of shadows across the
illuminated buildings seems to
breathe new life into these forms,
completely redesigning the
spaces inhabited by statues
created by eminent artists, such
as Bruno Giorgi's The Warriors.

The Metropolitan Cathedral

BRASÍLIA, BRAZIL

The Metropolitan Cathedral in Brasília is considered the most important expression of the inventiveness of its architect, Oscar Niemeyer. Its cornerstone was laid on September 12, 1958, and the basic groundwork completed in 1960, at which time sixteen concrete pillars surrounded by a 230-foot-diameter area were its only visible elements. The pillars have a parabolic cross section, and each one weigh 99 tons. Viewed as a whole, they represent hands folded in prayer and raised towards heaven.

In 1967 the cathedral, though still under construction, was given historic landmark status. This is because the city administration wanted to finish the construction work but could not use public funds, as religious works had to be financed by the Church and not the national government. Therefore, the administrative got around this by declaring the cathedral a historic monument, thus making it possible to use government funds to complete the project. (The cathedral was consecrated on May 31, 1970.)

On the square near the entrance, there are four ten-foot-tall bronze statues of the Evangelists arranged asymmetrically, with three to the left of the entrance and one to the right. The Brazilian sculptor Alfredo Ceschiatti completed them in 1968.

Next to the cathedral is the bell tower, which is a modernist reinterpretation of this traditional structure. It is composed of a support pillar that evokes the ones used in the cathedral, and it holds four large bells that were a gift from Spain.

The entire liturgical space is below ground level and is accessed through a dark, narrow corridor made of concrete and black granite. In contrast to the brooding aura of the dark corridor, the large nave (131 feet wide and 230 feet long) is flooded with light that shines through the windows and dome, and is reflected on the white marble surfaces. The dome windows are made of clear glass, although the original plans called for stained glass. The windows between the 16 columns are triangular, measuring 33 feet across the base and rising to a height of nearly 100 feet. The predominant colors are blue, white and brown, and the designs are the work of Marianne Peretti (1990).

Three angels, also the work of Ceschiatti, hang from thin steel cables suspended from the posts of the dome. The smallest statue is just over 7 feet tall and weighs 220 pounds, the medium one is 11 feet tall and weighs 440 pounds, and the largest one is 14 feet tall and weighs 660 pounds.

The uniformity of the cathedral is broken up by 13 chapels and the oval baptistery, and it is decorated with *azulejos*, typical Portuguese ceramic tiles designed by Athos Bulcão (1977).

The altar was given to the city by Pope Paul VI. The image of the patron saint of Brazil, Our Lady of Aparecida, is a replica of the original, located in the city of Aparecida do Norte in the State of São Paulo.

Paintings depicting the Way of the Cross, by Di Cavalcanti, cover one of the marble walls encircling the nave. On the marble column next to the entrance, Athos Bulcão painted several episodes from the life of the Virgin Mary. Inside the crypt, there is a replica of the Shroud of Turin. In discussing the cathedral, Niemeyer himself emphasizes its differences with respect to traditional churches. "Here, for example, I avoided the conventional solution of old, dark cathedrals, which evoke sin. Instead, I created a dark gallery leading to the nave, which is dazzling, colorful and vaulted, with beautiful clear windows opening up to infinity." (Alessandra Di Marco)

294 In constructing the cathedral, Niemeyer wanted to evoke structural tension united with the spiritual power of Gothic cathedrals. The 16 pillars, originally made of bare concrete, have recently been finished with special white paint.

DESIGN	CONSTRUCTION	DIMENSIONS	USE
O. Nyemeier	1958-1960	Total area 41,441 square ft	Church

294-295 The church is accessed via an underground ramp guarded by statues of the evangelists. Niemeyer designed it in order to accentuate the contrast between the darkness of the corridor and the radiance of the sanctuary, creating an architectural promenade representing the soul's path to redemption.

295 bottom The cathedral is surrounded by a ring of water, a symbolic purifying threshold that worshippers must cross before entering the liturgical setting.

296-297 The nave, viewed from the interior, seems to be flooded with light, dappled by the dazzling colors of the stained-glass windows.

BIBLIOGRAPHY

Ambasz, Emilio. *Emilio Ambasz: The poetics of the pragmatic*, Rizzoli International Publications, New York, 1988.

Andreu, Paul. *La Grande Arche Tête Défense, Paris-la-Défense: Une architecture de Johan Otto von Spreckelsen*, Editions du Demi-Cercle, Paris 1989.

Ballhausen, Nils. "DG-Bank, Berlin, Allemagne," in *L'architecture d'Aujourd'hui*, No. 335/July-August 2001, Paris.

Boissière, Olivier. "La Hong Kong & Shanghai Bank," in *L'Arca Plus*, no. 1/June 2004, Milan.

Bonet, Llorenc. *Jean Nouvel*, teNeues, Düsseldorf 2002.

Briganti, Antonio. "Il gigante d'oriente," in *Costruire* No. 248/January 2004, Milan.

Bruschi, Andrea and Dominique Perrault. *Architettura assente*, Edizioni Kappa, Rome 2002.

Buchanan, Peter. *Renzo Piano Building Workshop*, Volumes 1, 2, 3 4, Phaidon Press, London 1993-2000.

Campi, Massimiliano. *Norman Foster: Il disegno per la conoscenza di strutture complesse e di geometrie pure*, Edizioni Kappa, Rome 2002.

Chew Khuan and Uschi Schmitt. *1001 Arabian nights at the Burj Al Arab*, ABC Millennium, Cyprus 2000.

Courtiau, Jean-Pierre. *La Grande Arche = The Great Arch: Otto von Spreckelsen, Paul Andreu*, Herme, Paris 1997.

Dal Co, Francesco, Kurt W. Forster and Hadley Soutter Arnold, *Frank O. Gehry: tutte le opere*, Electa, Milan 1998.

Donin, G. and Renzo Piano. *Pezzo per pezzo/Piece by piece*, Casa del libro, Bari 1982.

Dorner, Elke. *Das Jüdische Museum Berlin*, Gebrüder Mann Verlag, Berlin 1999.

Pizzi, Emilio. *Renzo Piano*, Birkhäuser, Basel 2002 – Zanichelli, Bologna 2002.

Fadda, Mariopaolo. *Walt Disney Concert Hall di Frank O. Gehry*, Clean, Naples 2004.

Fessy, Georges. *Institut du Monde Arabe: une architecture de Jean Nouvel, Gilbert Lezenes, Pierre Soria, Architecture Studio*, Editions du Demi-Cercle, Paris 1989.

Foster, Norman. *Reflections / Norman Foster*, Prestel, London and Munich 2005.

Friedman, Mildred (ed.). *Frank O. Gehry: architettura + sviluppo – Frank O. Gehry and associates*, Rizzoli International, New York 1999.

Fuchs, Rudi H. "A place for art," in *A + U: A Monthly Journal of World Architecture and Urbanism*, No. 1985, Tokyo.

Gargiani, Roberto. *Idea e costruzione del Louvre, Saggi e documenti di storia dell'architettura*, Alinea, Florence 1998.

Glancey, Jonathan. "Museum Mönchengladbach, West Germany," in *Architectural Review*, No. 1030/1982, London.

Jodidio, Philip, *Piano. Renzo Piano Building Workshop 1966-2005*, Taschen, Cologne 2005.

Lampugnani, V.M. *Renzo Piano. Progetti e architetture 1964-1983; Progetti e Architetture 1984-1986; Progetti e Architetture 1987-1994*, Electa, Milan 1994.

Lauterbach, H., V. Leti Messina and M. Taut, *Hans Scharoun*, Officina, Rome 1970.

Lenci, Ruggero. "I.M. Pei. Teoremi spaziali," *Testo & Immagine*, Collana Universale di Architettura, Venice 2005.

Libeskind, Daniel. "Imperial War Museum," in *Area*, No. 65/2002, Milan.

Libeskind Daniel, *The Jewish Museum Berlin*, Verlag der Kunst, Berlin 1999.

Mikami, Yuzo. *Utzon's Sphere: Sydney Opera House – How it was designed and built*, Shokokusha, Tokyo 2001.

Molinari, Luca and Massimiliano Fuksas, *Massimiliano Fuksas: 1995-2005*, Skira, Milan 2005.

Murray, Peter. *The Saga of Sydney Opera House: The Dramatic Story of the Design and Construction of the Icon of Modern Australia*, Spon Press, London 2004.

Nobel, Philip. "Special issue. The hotel issue," in *Interiors*, Vol. 159, No. 6/June 2000.

Oddo, Maurizio. *La chiesa di Padre Pio a S. Giovanni Rotondo*, Motta Editore, Milan 2005.

Pavan, Vincenzo. "Edificio per uffici isolato, Berlino," in *Area* No. 55/March-April 2001, Milan.

Pawley, Martin. *Norman Foster: A Global Architecture*, Universe Publishing, New York 1999.

Pettena, Gianni. *Hans Hollein, opere 1960-1988*, Idea Books, Milan 1988.

Piano, Renzo. *Dialoghi di cantiere*, Laterza, Bari 1986.

Piano, Renzo. *Giornale di bordo* (reprint), Passigli Editore, Florence 2005.

Piano, Renzo. *On Tour with Renzo Piano*, Phaidon Press, London 2005.

Polano, Sergio. *Santiago Calatrava*, Electa Mondadori, Milan 1996.

Renzo Piano & Building Workshop, *Renzo Piano & Building Workshop*, Tormena Editore, Genoa 2004.

Riley, T. (ed.). *Architettura naturale: Emilio Ambasz, progetti e oggetti*, Electa, Milan 1999.

Sacchi, Livio. *Daniel Libeskind, Museo ebraico, Berlino*, Testo & Immagine, Turin 1998.

Saggio, Antonino. *Frank Owen Gehry: architetture residuali*, Testo & Immagine, Turin 1997.

Salam, Sami. "Istituto del Mondo Arabo," in *Abacus*, Vol. 3, No. 8/April 1987, Milan.

Schulz, Bernard. *The Reichstag: The Parliament Building by Norman Foster*, Prestel, Munich, London, New York 2000.

Segantini, Maria Alessandra. *Auditorium Parco della Musica*, Federico Motta Editore, Milan 2004.

Trasi, Nicoletta. "Tutto accade 'dentro' D.G. Bank in Berlin," in *L'Arca*, No. 166/January 2002, Milan.

Tzonis, Alexander. *Santiago Calatrava: The Complete Works*, Rizzoli, Milan 2004.

Underwood, David. *Oscar Niemeyer and the Architecture of Brazil*, Rizzoli International Publications, New York 1994.

Von Spreckelsen, Johann Otto. "Johann Otto von Spreckelsen: l'Arche de la Défense," in *Architektur DK*, No. 1-2/1990, Copenhagen

Werner, Frank. *Coop Himmelblau*, Birkhäuser, Basel 2000.

William, Stephanie. *Hong Kong Bank: The Building of Norman Foster's Masterpiece*, Little Brown, Boston 1989.

INDEX

PHOTO CREDITS

Courtesy of Moshe Safdie/Canadian Architecture Collection: pages 248 top

Liane Cary/Agefotostock/Marka: pages 268 top, 272-273

Stefano Cellai/Agefotostock/Marka: pages 230-231

Robert César/Artedia: page 72 left

Jèan-Marc Charles/Agefotostock/Marka: pages 66-67

Dave Collins/Agefotostock/Marka: page 20 bottom

Courtesy of CoopHimmelb(l)au: pages 114 center and bottom, 115, 116 top and bottom, 116-117, 118, 119 top, center and bottom, 121 bottom left and right

Peter Cook/VIEW: pages 22, 23 center and bottom

Stéphane Couturier/Artedia: pages 56-57, 57 top, center and bottom left, 58-59, 59 center and bottom, 60, 61, 65

John Crall/Agefotostock/Marka: pages 286-287

Marco Cristofori/Corbis: page 140 bottom

Pedro Luz Cunha/Alamy: page 290 center

Michel Denancé/Artedia: pages 44, 45, 50-51, 51 center and bottom, 53 top, center and bottom, 72-73, 74 bottom left and destra, 243, 244 bottom, 245, 246, 247 bottom

Patrik Durand/Corbis Sygma: page 43 bottom

Edifice/Corbis: pages 140-141

Georges Fessy/Artedia: pages 68 top, 70 center and bottom

Geogers Fessy/Ateliers Jean Nouvel: pages 54-55

Firefly Productions/Corbis: page 96

Kevin Fitzimons courtesy of Wexner Center for the Arts: pages 274-275, 276

Floto+Warner Studio: pages 258, 259 bottom left and center, 260 top, 260-261

Focus Team: page 64 top

Courtesy of Foster & Patners: pages 32 top and bottom, 33, 34-35, 35 top and center, 35 bottom left and right, 36 bottom, 37 top left and right, 37 bottom, 38, 39 top and bottom, 40 bottom left and right, 94 bottom, 95 bottom, 99 bottom left, 200 left and right, 206 bottom

Klaus Frahm/Artur: pages 84-85, 87 top, 92 bottom, 114 top, 120 top and bottom, 120-121

Galli/Laif/Contrasto: pages 90-91, 90 bottom

Olivier Martin Gambler/Artedia: pages 46-47

Ron Garnett/Airscapes: page 248 center

Chris Gascoigne/VIEW: page 20 top

Marc Gerritsen/Arcaid.co.uk: pages 210, 211 top, 211 bottom left and right, 212 left and right, 213, 214, 215 top, bottom left and right

Dennis Gilbert/VIEW: pages 16-17, 29, 39 center, 40 top, 51 top, 85 bottom left and right, 89 bottom, 98, 101 top, 135 left, 137 top and bottom, 138-139, 216-217, 217 left and right, 218-219, 219, 223, 224 top and bottom, 224-225, 225 bottom left and right

Reinhard Gorner/Artur: pages 82-83, 87 center, 88-89

Charles Grust/Danita Delimont: pages 254-255

Grafenhain Gunter/Sime/Sie: pages 100-101

Ronald Halbe/Artur: pages 83 bottom, 88 bottom, 106 bottom left

Roland Halbe/Artur/VIEW: pages 14, 102 top, center and bottom, 102-103, 103 bottom, 104, 105 top, 105 bottom left and destra, 106 bottom right, 107

Paul Hardy/Corbis: pages 36-37

J.D.Heaton/Agefotostock/Marka: page 233

Karin Hesmann/Artur: pages 134-135

Karin Hesmann/Artur/VIEW: pages 122 top and bottom, 123, 124 top, center and bottom, 124-125, 126, 127 top and bottom

Christian Heeb/Hemispheres: page 292 bottom left and right

Christian Heeb/Laif/Contrasto: page 289

Jochen Helle/Artur: pages 110-111, 112-113, 113 top and center

Jurgen Henkelmann/Artur: pages 106 top

Hermes/Agefotostock/Marka: page 91 bottom

Jon Hicks/Corbis: pages 96-97, 101 center

Courtesy of Atelier Hans Hollein: page 108 bottom

Andrew Holt/Alamy: page 31 center

Fred Housel courtesy of The Seattle Public Library: page 256

Wolfgang Hoyt/Esto: page 274 bottom

Courtesy of Franz Hubmann/Atelier Hans Hollein: page110 bottom

Hufton & Crow/VIEW: pages 21 bottom left and right, 41, 269 bottom

Courtesy of Greg Hursley/Emilio Ambasz & Associates: pages 278 top and bottom, 279, 280 top and bottom, 281 bottom

Timothy Hursley: 251 bottom right, 252-253, 253 right top and bottom

Wernar Huthmacher/Artur: page 99 top

Icponline/Topfoto/Hip: page 295 bottom

Imaginechina/Picture-Alliance: page 208 top and bottom left

Satoshi Isono/Architectural Association: pages 288-289, 290 bottom

Joergensen/Laif/Contrasto: pages 92 center, 92-93

M. Christopher Jones courtesy of Wexner Center for The Arts: page 275 top

Courtesy of Jumeirah International: pages 199 top and bottom

JW/Masterfile/Sie: page 206 top

Wolfgang Kaehler/Corbis: page 250

Erika Koch/Artur: pages 86-87

Ian Lambot: pages 201, 202, 203 top and bottom, 204, 205 bottom

Langrock/Zenit/Laif/Contrasto: page 82 bottom

Javier Larrea/Agefotostock/Contrasto: page 140 top

Dirk Laubner: page 196 top

Julien Le Cordier/Hoa-Qui/HachettesPhotos/Contrasto: page 59 top

Dieter Leistner/Artur: pages 68-69

Yadid Levy/Alamy: page 198

R.Ian Lloyd/Masterfile/Sie: pages 207, 240 bottom, 241

John Edward Linden/Arcaid.co.uk: pages 92 top

Miquel Tres Lopez/Agefotostock/Marka: page 91 top

Attar Maher/Corbis Sygma/Corbis: page 197

Joe Malone/Sime/Sie: pages 294-295

Rafael Macia/Agefotostock/Marka: page 283 bottom

Maurizio Marcato: pages 2-3, 166-167, 166 bottom, 167 top and bottom,168 top, 169,170, 171 top, bottom left and right

James Marshall/Corbis: pages 236-237

Andre Maslennikov/Agefotostock/Marka: page 196 bottom left

Courtesy of Foto Mayska: pages 108-109

Michel Moch: page 294

Michel Moch/Artedia: pages 288 bottom left, 290 top, 292-293

Florian Monheim/Artur: page 113 bottom

Courtesy of National Gallery of Canada: page 251 top

Mike Olenick courtesy of Wexner Center for the Arts: page 277

D G Olshavsky: page 275 bottom

Courtesy of OMA and OMA-LMN: pages 255 bottom, 257 bottom, 259 top and bottom right, 260 center

Courtesy of Ateliers Jean Nouvel: pages 55 bottom, 57 bottom right

Catherine Panchout/Corbis: page 87 bottom

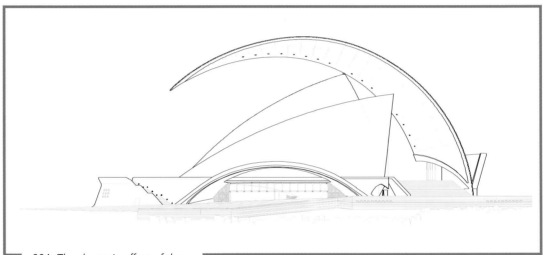

304 The dramatic effect of the
two external "sails" is evident in
the cross section of Calatrava's
Tenerife Opera House. These
imaginary waves dialogue with
the real ones of the ocean in
front of the concert hall.

Courtesy of Cesar Pelli& Associates: pages 226 top and bottom left and right, 229

Perkovic/Laif/Contrasto: pages 108 top, 111 top and bottom

Courtesy of Renzo Piano Building Workshop: pages 1, 42 top and bottom, 182 top, 222 top and bottom, 242 bottom right, 244 top

Puku/Sime/Sie: pages 228, 230 bottom

PLC/Alamy: page 27 top

Louie Psihoyos/Corbis: page 208 bottom right

José Fuste Raga/Agefotostock/ Contrasto: page 147 bottom

José Fuste Raga/Corbis: pages 151 center, 194 bottom, 232-233

Paul Raftery/VIEW: pages 134 bottom, 136-137, 182 bottom, 182-183, 183 bottom

Rainer Rehfeld/Artur: page 240 top

Paolo Riolzi: page 180 top

RMN Photo: pages 62-63

Courtesy of Richard Rogers Partnership: pages 24 top and bottom right, 27 bottom left and right, 31 top and bottom, 43 top, 46, 49 bottom

Paolo Rosselli/Studio di Fotografia Milano courtesy of Santiago

Calatrava: pages 78-79

Laurent Rousseau/Top/HachettePhotos/ Contrasto: pages 43 bottom, 52-53

Courtesy of Philippe Ruault: pages 179 center

Philippe Ruault: pages 254, 256-257, 257 top, 259 center, 260 bottom

Ted Soqui/Corbis: pages 268 bottom, 270 top, 270 top, center and bottom, 271

Top Foto: page 295 bottom

Edmund Summer/View: pages 188, 189 right

Hiroyasu Sakaguchi: pages 216 bottom, 220 top and bottom, 221

Neil Setchfield/Lonely Planet Images: page 9

Reinhard Schmid/Sime/Sie: page 195

Doug Scott/Agefotostock/Marka: pages 286-287, 290-291

Giovanni Simeone/Sime/Sie: pages 131 bottom, 234-235

Skyscan/Corbis: page 194 top

Grant Smith/VIEW: page 37 center

Courtesy of Studio Snohetta S.A.: pages 190 top, 190 bottom right, 190-191, 191 bottom

James Sparshatt/Corbis: pages 146-147

Herbert Spichtinger/Zefa/Corbis: page 239 bottom

State Library of New South Wales: pages 236 top, 237 bottom, 238 bottom, 239 top

Barbara Staubach/Artur: page 28 top

Stiftung Archiv Der Akademie der Künste: page 84 bottom, 85 top

Ken Straiton/Corbis: page 97 bottom

Juergen Stumpe: pages 18-19, 141 bottom left and right, 151 top

Ulana Switucha/Alamy: pages 196 bottom right

A.Tondini/Focus Team: pages 149 bottom left and right, 285 top

William Vassal courtesy of Renzo Piano Building Workshop: page 247 top

Giulio Veggi/Archivio White Star: pages 69 bottom, 237 right top and bottom, 238-239

Michael S. Yamashita/Corbis: pages 4-5

Anthony Weller/Architectural Association: page 30

Henry Westheim/Alamy: page 231

Peter.M.Wilson/Corbis: pages 296-297

Jeremy Woodhouse/Masterfile/Sie: pages 94, 209

Worldwilde Picture Library/Alamy: page 293

ACKNOWLEDGEMENTS

The authors and the publisher are grateful to the following architectural firms:

Emilio Ambasz and Associates, especially Brad Whitermore
Mario Botta Architetto, especially Elisiana Di Bernardo
Coop Himmelb(l)au
Santiago Calatrava SA, especially Angelika Kreuzer
Eisenman Architects, especially Matthew Ford
Massimiliano Fuksas Architetto, especially Ms. Luccioli
Hans Hollein Atelier, especially Madeleine Jenewein
Foster and Partners, especially Kathryn Tollervey
Jean Nouvel Atelier, especially Charlotte Kruk
Office for Metropolitan Architecture, especially David van der Leer
Pelli Clarke Pelli, especially Ben Charney
Dominique Perrault Architecture, especially Raffaella Faccioli
Renzo Piano Building Workshop, especially Chiara Casazza and Stefania Canta
Richard Rogers Partnership, especially Jenny Stephens
Moshe Safdie and Associates, especially Laura Jackson
Snøhetta
and Andrea Bruno